Mom Mumbles and Pop Can't Pee

*A Real Life Adventure
with Aging Parents*

Peter Christian Olsen

**LUCAS
PARK
BOOKS**

ST. LOUIS, MISSOURI

Permissions were given to include quotes and sections from the following: *New Revised Standard Version Bible,* copyright 1989, Division of Christian Education of the National Council of the Churches of Christ in the United States of America. Used by permission. All rights reserved.

Koenig, Harold G., "Religion and Health in Later life," *Aging, Spirituality and Religion: A Handbook,* Melvin Kimble, ed., p. 9.

Price, Christine A., *Tips When Visiting a Nursing Home, (SS-188-01)*

Lee, Michael, author of "How To Be An Expert Persuader...In 20 Days or Less"

Everett, Deborah, *Forget me not: the spiritual care of people with Alzheimer's,* Inkwell Press, Edmonton, 1996, p. 167.

Print ISBN: 9781603500302

Published by Lucas Park books
www.lucasparkbooks.com

Printed in the United States of America

Contents

Introduction

Life Does Not Allow Do-overs

Where can I go from your spirit?
Or where can I flee from your presence?
If I ascend to heaven, you are there;
If I make my bed in Sheol, you are there.
If I take the wings of the morning
And settle at the furthest limits of the sea,
Even there your hand shall lead me,
and your right hand shall hold me fast.
If is say, "surely the darkness shall cover me,
And the light around me become night,"
Even the darkness is not dark to you;
The night is as bright as the day,
For darkness is as light to you......Psalm 139, vs. 7-12

Hindsight is always sharper than foresight. Monday morning quarterbacks have a distinct advantage. It is unbelievable how knowledgeable and insightful people can be the next day after a game. The perspective afterwards can be much clearer than the perspective beforehand. I can't count the number of times in my own life I have muttered in disgust, "If I only knew before what I know now, things would have been drastically different."

It's the "do over" mentality. As a child I quickly grasped the power of the "do over." It had a certain prominence and dominion over the laws of space and time. I shouted "do over" frequently any time I wasn't prepared for the game to begin or I missed a point or made a wrong turn or wasn't ready for the next pitch or felt I got a late start in the race. I never hesitated to exert my influence for upholding the natural born right to do over what I had gotten wrong the first time. As one friend remarked, "do overs can make the difference between making a mistake and being one."

1

High school, for instance, is one experience I often wish I could do over. I remember it as one big blunder after another. I wasn't ready then, but I am now. A recurring dream I have is of returning to my high school some fifty years later. I have the body of a teenager but the moxey and wisdom of a sixty-five year old. Life suddenly becomes wonderful. I bask in my own "coolness" as captain of the soccer team. I share my "fonzy" acquired wisdom with the naïve students and they are duly impressed. Most of all, I have no fear of asking the head cheerleader to the Saturday night dance.

Some of my wishes for "do overs" reflect regrets for things I have done and wished I hadn't – taking that first puff on a cigarette, forgetting to use a condom, eating the largest hamburger McDonald's sells, day dreaming in physics class. Then there are things I left undone and wished I hadn't – not flossing my teeth often enough, not learning to play the piano, abandoning Spanish lessons, failing to study for my high school English final. I yearn for a chance to do these over again.

Hindsight is the mother of regret. Thomas Wolfe once remarked that a person "can't go home again." Only the hopelessly innocent fail to recognize that you can't go back and change things that have already happened. To consume your allotted time and energy left of this earth worrying about "what might have happened if only" or "what you should have done instead" leads to a downward spiral of pathos and remorse from which you might never climb back out. Too much attention paid to "do overs" diverts energy from making a difference in the future, but the temptation is overwhelming. The possibility of "do overs" continuously haunts my thoughts

Both my parents are gone now. My father passed away ten years ago and my mother shortly thereafter. For the last decade of their lives, I was their primary care taker. As I reflect on this experience, I wish for the chance to do it all over again, but differently, radically differently.

I wasn't their sole care taker. I had help from my wife, my brothers, assisted living staff, hospice, and other medical personnel. But I was the primary person, the one who made the decisions about where they would live, provided regular visitation, handled the frequent emergencies, and resolved the unending problems. Both Mom and Pop came to rely heavily upon me to make significant determinations about what circumstances would best provide a quality of life for their remaining years. They often didn't agree, but respected my opinion and usually submitted to my suggestions.

I didn't ask to be their caretaker. It was thrust upon me. I moved into this responsibility reluctantly, but obligingly and willingly. I could not ignore my responsibility. I found it hard to imagine that any adult child looks forward with great anticipation and glee to becoming parent to his parents, but how could I refuse? Lurking in the recesses of my mind was the vivid recollection of how my parents assumed responsibility for me during my growing years. I had tortured them with the many small and not so small annoyances of adolescence. I added anxiety to their lives by not always following their rules. When I jeopardized my future it caused them immeasurable grief. Despite these difficulties, they continued to feed me, cloth me, educate me, nurture me, and support me. They never abandoned me. How could I now abandon them? It was quid pro quo. With much fear and trepidation, I undertook the task of becoming parent to my parents. It was not to be an easy task.

I never made intentional plans to be parent to my parents. As a matter of fact, I don't remember even thinking about that possibility prior to the time it was thrust upon me. Like most people in the same or similar situations, becoming caretaker of your parents happens without a lot of forethought. It just happens. One day they are independent people living on their own somewhere out there in retirement la la land. Then suddenly, without warning, Mom takes a terrible tumble or Pop gets too old and gives up driving or some debilitating disease attacks one of them and the other claims not to be able to take care of the sick one alone and the next day (or perhaps week or month) they are in need of assisted living. It wasn't anticipated, at least not right then. Of course, being a realist, you always considered that some day your parents would get old and would need some assistance, but that wa⁻

sometime in the distant future. at a different age and stage in life, much further along down the road.

Eventually that time comes. The fall that Mom had demands attention now. Since Pop no longer drives, somebody has to get their food. People at every age still eat three times each day. Neither parent can remember much about what they did yesterday, it would be cruel to ignore the symptoms of senility until their forgetfulness becomes the cause of a serious accident, like failing to wash dishes or turning off the stove, or taking baths or turning off the outside water hose or burning the house down. These circumstances can't be put off for a more convenient time. They need to be addressed now, immediately.

Most of the time when a family moved to a new location, considerable thought went into planning. If it involved a new job that required a move to a new town, they researched the location, found the best school systems, considered where taxes were the least, and thought about what size house and in which neighborhood was best suited for your chosen life style. Perhaps some moving manuals were consulted and a real estate agent was employed.

That's not the case with aging parents. When parents show signs of deterioration, it often comes as a surprise, quickly, and without warning. Time is at a minimal for planning the next step. Consulting with experts, reading senior care manuals, and preplanning often have to take a backseat to present priorities like finding a place for Mom and Pop to live with services that are needed immediately.

That's what happened to me. It was a decision made spontaneously to move my parents from their totally independent living arrangements in another state far away to an assisted living facility at a location near to my home. The simple act of moving them carried with it the assumption that I would become a primary player, if not the single provider in their caretaking. Once that move was made and those services were begun, it wasn't long before the whole focus of my parents life was focused on increasing the services and assuming more of the responsibility for their care.

In retrospect, I now wish I could do it all over again. It's not that I enjoyed the experience; that it was so pleasant and inspirational a time in our lives that I can't wait for it to happen again. Rather it's knowing that I made many mistakes I wish I could un-do. The guilt factor sometimes feels overwhelming. Too many times I misunderstood and misinterpreted their feelings and circumstances. I discounted their real fears. I underestimated their needs. I never fully comprehended their mental attitudes or encouraged their reliance on spiritual resources that might have provided relief and focus. In short, I was entirely unprepared to assume the task of parenting to my parents. Even harder is to accept that I can't do it over again.

It was a difficult time for me and I think I made it even more difficult for them. Their dream was that old age would be a time of peace and contentment. With great difficulty and unrealized expectations, the sought only that they might find comfort, serenity, and contentedness during their remaining years. I never quite understood that nor comprehended how that might happen for them. I was not able to find the "handle" to managing their discontentment. Their physical health took its toll as they aged, but not nearly as much as their emotional well being. I allowed their spiritual health to remain elusive.

Now I wish for a do over. When I reflect on those tumultuous years and recognize the mistakes I made, the opportunities I missed, and the challenges I left undone that could have added serenity and tranquility to their remaining years that I could have provided emotional stability, I only wish I could do it over. I don't relish the thought of once again living through their unhappiness, emotional distress, and discontent, but I do wish that I would have had the knowledge and insight I now have about how it could have been a better experience.

I wish I could relate an experience of parenting my parents that held great potential as a time in both our lives, a time that proved to be vibrant and full of fond memories, a time we both cherished and never wanted to see end. Unfortunately that was not the case. This was a time of unrelenting anxiety, depression, and emotional turmoil on both our parts, theirs as they faced the challenges of old age, and mine as I faced the challenges of parenting my parents.

So many times since their demise, I have wondered aloud; questioned if my actions then were for their benefit or my own. I wish now that I was more aware of the significant role spirituality plays in older people and was better able to apply these insights to provide for their contentment with the aging process. I missed these opportunities, either through ignorance or intentionally or both. It's now too late to do over again.

As I think back upon those years, I now recognize that role of spirituality, or the lack of it, is a major factor affecting the success of the aging process. Healthy spirituality can be the difference maker in a person's life; the difference between a life of joy and delight or one of utter despair. Spirituality is not merely a synonym for religion. Each person's approach to spirituality is independent of their religious perspective. For some religious is the focus. For others, religion has no bearing. Either way, one's ability to recognize and utilize spiritual resources adds a dimension to the quality of one's life.

A person's spirituality is linked to their sense of identity. Spiritual well being is the affirmation of life in relationship with God, self, community, and the environment. It is not one dimensional; rather it permeates and gives meaning to the whole of life. It is the mechanism by which a person gains strength, understanding, confidence and reassurance. It enables the person to let go of despair, grief, fear, and guilt and reach for something curative, something that will enhance the caliber and character of living.

We each experience spirituality personally and uniquely. It requires individualized abstract thinking and will. It is the dimension of the personality that integrates all other aspects of personhood. Spirituality is like a well that one taps when the need arises to overcome loss and adjust to change. It provides the healing attitude one brings to problems. For many people the spiritual life *is* the religious life. Yet, one can summon up the spiritual without being religious.

Everyone has a spiritual component, but not everyone is religious. Neither of my parents was particularly religious.

Perhaps that is where I misconstrued my approach as their caretaker. Although I never felt comfortable with a religious vocabulary in their presence I still failed to recognize and acknowledge they had a spiritual side despite their indifference to things religious. Even those few times when their spiritual nature became apparent and important, I failed to respond out of ignorance or fear or both.

Both of my parents suffered through periods of mental anguish during the last decade of their lives. For my father, it was extreme anxiety. He just never succeeded in being the happy camper he so desired. Satisfaction, peace, and contentment eluded him. Nothing I could do or provide was ever able to overcome his constant frustration and disgruntlement over growing older. The role of spirituality and its focus on introspection and personal resolution seemed to always be a issue that remained in the abstract and on the sidelines, but never the focus. He sought peace and contentment from resources outside himself rather than from those within him. His spirituality remained undiscovered and unexploited.

Mom contracted dementia. After years of physical and mental neglect, not the least of which was alcoholism and an addiction to medications, she succumbed to severe dementia. Dementia carries with it special problems, including but not limited to memory loss and the inability to hold meaningful and coherent conversations. Once a person falls captive to the ravishes of dementia in its many and varied forms, and is no longer capable of rational thinking and clear communication of thoughts, we often dismiss that person from our normal relations. We treat the person as if they were childlike; incapable of adult feelings and lacking mature understanding. We assume that if the person can't converse about their spirituality then they have no spirituality. Such was the circumstances that characterized my relationship with Mom. Her evolving dementia so epitomized her personality that I never felt comfortable about dealing with her spirituality.

Throughout the mental demise of both my parents, I encountered personal difficulties both recognizing the distressing symptoms and even more important, responding appropriately to these symptoms. My father's constant complaining and discontent with everything about his life those last years, I chalked up to his just being a crouch and curmudgeon. Mom's creeping dementia caused her to become Pop's greatest agitation. Her bizarre behaviors colored her relationships with all people in her environment, including myself. The concept that each remained fully a person with dignity demanding respect and understanding was often lost as I attempted to acquiesce to their needs and demands with as minimal disruption of my own life as possible.

The person with dementia is still a person, albeit with limited capacity, but with full acumen of feelings, thoughts, and behaviors. Spirituality is not an aspect of life reserved only for the fully functional. To be alive is to be spiritual. What does the person with dementia need? Essentially much the same attributes accorded to the fully functional including feelings of connectedness, competency, usefulness, success and love.

These attributes are what comprise the spiritual life of any person. My mother and father were no exceptions. If I were particularly alert to this aspect of their lives, I could have contributed greatly to that which would have proved helpful in caring for them – the true meaning of their personalities, what comforted them in times of grief and despair, what gave them encouragement throughout their struggles, where they could find resolve to handle defeat, fear, and confusion.

For the person with dementia, however, discovering their level of spirituality is greatly diminished. Since conversation and communication are limited or eliminated completely, the normal routes for introspection, discovery, and insight are all but eliminated. The person with dementia can not articulate what concerns them, what their hopes for the future might be, or what concerns they are experiencing with daily life. Hence, for my mother this always remained an issue I ignored.

Life with my parents during the last decade of their lives was a tumultuous one. I entered the care taking phase without prior knowledge. Like a first time father with no instructional manual about child care, being a parent to my parents was an exercise of groping in the abyss. I was going down a dark hallway I had never been down before. Lots of monsters lay hidden in the crevices and corners. It was a learn by doing experience. Unfortunately they died before all the learning happened.

Hundreds of thousands of people each year enter into similar situations with their own parents or loved ones. There exists innumerable manuals and similar how to books concerned with the proper way to care for aging parents. I have since read a good many of them and they can be helpful. And yet, going down that road remains a personal experience, a unique adventure for each family. How to manuals might give excellent advice about dealing with certain circumstances and consequences related to the aging process, but such advice comes as preparation beforehand and often generic in scope. No manual can possible anticipate each families unique situation or adequately explain every experience you are likely to confront.

This was a difficult time for me as well as for my family. I often felt extremely conflicted. Despite that the demands on my time as caretaker were minimal; those times that I did spend were not often quality times. It did not work out that the remaining years of my parents were a time to reconnect, to explore their alternatives for the future, to participate in positive recollections, and to re establish positive relationships. Instead, I remember them as time of active involvement helping a time of crisis, a time of sorting out options for them, a time of worry about their physical and mental health, and a time of choices for resolving a myriad of obstacles and problems that confounded them daily. It was work, make no mistake about that.

Guilt entered the equation often. Because time spent with them was not always pleasant time, I carried a feeling of obligation which was a different feeling than looking forward to quality time spent with them. Perhaps it was the anticipation of having to resolve their constant and repeated problems that kept me at a distance. At the same time, I also felt that I needed to spend more time with them if for no other reason than their time left was at a minimal. Whenever

I felt pressured or under obligation, I often wished that death would come sooner rather than later so that I might be relieved of my obligation. I am not proud of these thoughts. I do wish for a do over.

Keeping life in balance was a priority. Devoting the necessary time to my parent's welfare and also devoting the time needed for family life was always on my mind. My children were mostly grown, but my wife and I enjoyed a very good relationship and wished to spend as much time together as possible. Work took its toll as well in terms of time allotted. The frustration of not being able to create for them a contented, peaceful existence upset me tremendously. I saw my task as "fixing" their lives, an experience impossible to achieve.

Too many times I felt sorry for myself; I felt that I had a burden that interfered in the pursuit of my happiness. Taking care of my parents did not produce happiness. I envisioned it as a responsibility I could not avoid. Although convinced that placing parents in a nursing home is not always a cruel event; that if one is relieved from daily care and maintenance of aging parents and transferring some of that responsibility to a nursing home staff, then presumably some time and energy would remain for re-establishing a relationship. This did not prove to be the case. Responsibility for my parents continued to feel like a burden to me and I never was quite able to shake that feeling .

It is the intent of this book to share with the reader my experience of being parent to my parents. Although truly a unique venture to me, but certainly parts of it will resonate with many others. The content is comprised of vignettes from regular and ongoing visits I shared with Mom and Pop. During the last decade of their lives, I visited with them almost weekly, sometimes even more frequently, while they lived in a variety of retirement settings – at homes in the country, at assisted living facilities, in mental hospitals, and in nursing homes. I shared with them many of their life experiences – sicknesses, hospital stays, holidays, shopping ventures, private conversations, arguments, and personal turmoil's. Sometimes I was invited in, other times I invited myself in. Rarely did anything occur in their lives during that last decade when I was not personally and intimately involved. I observed and responded to my mother's slow demise into dementia. I confronted my father's extreme anxiety. I witnessed both of their deaths.

Rather than offer advice to the reader, instead I share experiences. It is my hope that the reader will glean a sense of life with aging parents and the demands of becoming a parent to your parents. It is an adventure of a life time.

1

One More Move and Then We're Done

"I don't believe one grows older. I think that what happens early in life is that at a certain age one stands still and stagnates."...T.S. Eliot.

The very first moment I arrived, I knew something had to change. At the time I wasn't sure what changes were needed, but I did know it was up to me to make them.

After a series of moves around the country looking for the idyllic retirement location, my mother and father ended up living in a trailer in North Carolina. I flew over from Texas and rented a car. At age seventy five, Pop was diagnosed with postrate cancer. He might have had the disease years previously, but the pain in his legs and his difficulty urinating became symptoms he couldn't ignore. An operation was scheduled. While Pop recovered in the hospital, I stayed with Mom.

As I entered the trailer, I immediately sensed catastrophe. Maybe I was over-reacting, but I noticed holes in the couch - small holes about the size of pennies. I looked around and saw other holes in the easy chair next to the lamp and still more holes in the cushions on the scattered furniture. I saw burn stains on the wooden side table.

"Mom," I asked. "How did these holes get in all your furniture?"

"What holes?" she responded. I could tell by the tone of her voice she knew exactly what holes to which I referred.

"All these small holes. The ones here on the couch and in that chair by the table," I said. I pointed them out to her. "They look like burn holes."

"Maybe some of them are," Mom said, "but it's nothing to worry about. Are you hungry? Do you want a peanut butter sandwich?" She tried her best to distract me.

"Mom, these are cigarette burns," I said. You and Pop drop ashes on the furniture."

As I examined the trailer more closely, I saw burned down cigarettes butts lying precariously on the edge of ash trays, by the side of the sink, and on the washing machine cover. Cigarettes had been lit and then abandoned lying half burned on whatever furniture was close by. They were lighting cigarettes and forgetting where they left them. I couldn't believe what I was seeing. How long, I wondered, before they burned themselves alive? Changes had to be made.

* * * *

The dream of "the golden years", the time of retirement, is often pure fantasy full of pipe dreams and unmet expectations. Too many people who dream of retirement as an idyllic and contented existence discover instead a time fraught with worry, frustration, insecurity, and disillusionment. Retirement is greatly over rated. Success depends upon one's attitudes and expectations. Pop had difficulty converting his attitudes and expectations into the reality of retirement.

Webster defines retirement as "a retreat, a withdrawal from one's occupation or from usual use of service." When retirement happens is inconsequential. What matters most is how the time is spent, what mental preparations have been made, what predilections and prejudices are carried into that life stage, and what hopes and notions are dragged along. Mom and Pop ignored these indicators by a country mile. They entered retirement completely unprepared.

Retirement went horribly wrong for both my parents. Retirement is a passage from one place to another, from one time to another time, from one stage in life to a new stage in life. It is to move from the comfortable and routine headlong toward the risky and precarious. It is intentional movement. To be a positive experience, it needs serious consideration before undertaking. It needs a plan and my father was without a plan. Pop was "forced" into retirement before he was ready by the unexpected leaving of his brother and partner in their business. He couldn't manage to run the business alone. Pop, as well as Mom, were unprepared for this journey. Their histories and past experience set them up for failure. Living in the trailer in North Carolina was just one more episode in my parent's long struggle to find peace and contentment in retirement. Overwhelming odds constantly plagued them. Their journey into retirement began in a small town in Vermont.

I took a small pastorate, my first church, in Southern Vermont right after graduating from theological school. When my father was forced to retire before he was ready, he bought a small house a few miles from where I was living and moved, lock, stock and barrel, from his home in New Jersey where they had lived for twenty-five years. Buried somewhere deep in his unconscious recesses, Pop had a mental picture of the idyllic small New England Village, the epitome of the contented and peaceful retirement location. That's where he intended to be and that's where he went.

Mom seemed excited about the move at first. I don't think she was included in the decision, but acquiesced nonetheless. It was not long, however, before the isolation of the small community began to weigh heavily on Mom's mental resources. She complained of loneliness and separation. She resented Pops routine of golfing, garden work, and visits with friends that excluded her. She stated she didn't want to go out, but I think it was a ruse, a passive/aggressive technique.

About six months after the move, Mom's rebellion began in earnest. She refused to can Pop's home grown vegetables. She would not prepare dinner at six o'clock which was Pop's routine. Housework was neglected. What she assumed were Pop's expectations of her, she purposefully ignored.

One day I got a call from my father. He sounded frantic. "Your mother is gone," he told me. He sounded frantic. "What do you mean gone? Where did she go? I asked.

"I don't know. She got mad about something, went out in the car, and I haven't heard from her in hours."

"What happened? I thought she didn't drive anymore?" I remarked.

"She never does," he said. "She didn't tell me she was taking the car. She just went outside and the next thing I knew the car was gone."

"I don't know what the hell is going on with you two," I told him. "Let me think where she might have gone and what I can do. I'll call you back." I was pissed.

"You know what she is like," Pop said. We both hung up.

Later that same evening, Mom called me.

"Where are you?" was my first question.

"I'm at a hotel in Hanover," she said.

"Are you alright?" I asked.

"I'm fine," she told me. "But I'm angry at your father."

She sounded confused or perhaps a little drunk. She didn't answer specifically why she left, but instead repeated vague insinuations about the attitudes of my father.

"He's crazy," she said. "I just don't want to be with him. He makes me feel shitty. I just wanted to leave." She expressed feeling hurt, but in a nonchalant manner.

"What are your plans?" I asked.

"I don't know. I'm a grownup and I can do what I want."

"I'm coming up there," I told her. "Stay right there until I get there." It was about a two hour drive to Hanover on the Vermont border.

"Never mind," she said.

"I'm coming anyway," I said. Immediately my mind began reminiscing about Moms history with mental instability.

Ten years earlier I was a senior in college. One day I received a call from my younger brother. He told me that Mom was behaving very funny, saying a lot of weird things, and acting crazy like. He sounded frightened. He didn't ask for help, but I could tell by his tone of voice that he was greatly concerned and confused.

I left college and went home. Mom's behavior had become truly bizarre. Both my father and brother knew something was wrong, but said little to her. Mom was very argumentative and particularly resented intrusions in her logic. She was extremely lethargic. She didn't shop for food, refused to do housework, stopped going to her club meetings, and just lay on the couch for hours during the day. We approached her about her behavior but she refused to acknowledge it.

"You can all go to hell," was her usual response.

Moment by moment her moods changed. She became totally unpredictable. She believed we were the enemy.

"You don't appreciate me," she told us. "You had better leave me alone and stay out of my way."

I suspected she was either on the verge of a mental breakdown or my imagination was running rampant; perhaps I was convincing myself that she was going crazy because her behavior didn't meet my expectations of "normal". Despite the increase in abnormal behavior and the constant barrage of verbal attacks on us, we remained in denial. Silently, we hoped that it was a passing phase.

Panic mode eventually set in. When her peculiar and erratic behavior passed the point of denial we felt forced to take action. With a constant barrage of appeals, we convinced Mom to see a doctor. He convinced her to enter Overbrook.

Overbrook was known in our community as the local insane asylum. We had no knowledge of the services they actually provided. The facilities resembled a college campus with gothic red brick buildings, connecting tunnels, dormitories, administration buildings, sprawling lawns, huge oak trees, and its own fire department. Overbrook resided there for decades as a county mental institution, but what happened there was largely unknown in the community.

Appearances can be deceiving. From the outside Overbrook looked peaceful and bucolic, a place to take a pleasant Sunday walk among its ornamental shrubs and across its spacious lawns. Inside the hospital resembled a prison. Heavy steel doors guarded the patient dormitory sections. Each door had a small opening through which an attendant could see and approve a visitor's pass. No privacy existed. Toilets had no doors and bedrooms no walls. No mirrors, no hooks, and no shades anywhere.

With a pass, we could go in, but Mom could not come out. Sometimes the attendants give patient updates. "Your Mom is doing well" or "She has been belligerent today," or "She takes her medications willingly," they would tell us. Most times the staff just grumbled incoherently as if questions about patients were an annoyance.

Mom sat in the sitting room when we visited. She was curled up with her legs under her. She wore a ratty bathrobe.

"Can I have a cigarette?" were her first words. She could smoke only under supervision. Conversation was limited.

"How are you feeling Mom," I asked her.

"Fine."

"Do you hurt anywhere?" I asked.

"No."

"Do you think they are helping you here?"

"I don't know what you are talking about."

I don't remember any consultation with a doctor. Only the attendants offered diagnosis.

"Your mother is a sick lady and needs to be here," they told me.

Therapy wasn't working at Overbrook. Mom was no worse, but not getting any better after three months in residency. A local physician we knew suggested we transfer Mom to a private mental hospital in South Jersey. They utilized shock treatment. We were told it was effective and safe. He told us it was the best option for someone in "her condition." We were not sure what "her condition" was, but she responded well to the shock treatment.

Mom came home one month later. I returned to college to complete my senior year. I went on to graduate school for four more years. My time home was limited to vacations. For the next few years, Mom appeared to live a normal life. She never expressed much joy, but neither did she experience much depression. All appeared well until retirement and the move to Vermont.

In the car on the way up to Hanover, I continued to reminisce about Mom's struggle with mental health issues. I realized that this episode was one more among a whole host of "slips" she had been having ever since Pop's retirement and the move from her old home in New Jersey.

When I arrived at the hotel, I encouraged her to talk with me. I wanted her to tell me what she was thinking. She was reluctant. It felt as if she thought it all just a lark, deserving of little consequence. Nothing in particular bothered her, she told me. She just felt like traveling.

"Will you come home now?" I asked her

"Maybe I will and maybe I won't," she replied. She had a smirk on her face. "But no promises."

I left her at the hotel. I felt my only option was to encourage her to come home and leave it up to her. The next day she returned home.

Three months later, Mom had an epiphany. She declared herself an alcoholic. She demanded immediate intervention. I was assigned the task of locating an adequate treatment center. She insisted it be a place where she could smoke. I found the perfect location.

After six weeks of "treatment", gallons of coffee, and cartons of cigarettes, Mom declared herself cured. I don't think she fully comprehended the concept of being an alcoholic. She returned to her home in Vermont.

The idyllic retirement life in Vermont proved too demanding for my parents. The next few years saw a continuous pilgrimage to different locations around the East coast searching for the best location – the coast of Maine, central Florida, and then back to New England. Always there were extenuating circumstances that proved overwhelming, conditions they could not adjust to, and emotional struggles that caused disappointment. Pop felt "forced" to move because of conditions, real or imaginary, he could not control or tolerate or caused extreme anxiety. Vermont winter ice built up on the roof and leaked down the walls and the well might go dry. Maine was too cold and too isolated and maybe the furnace might fail. Florida weather was too warm in summer and the drain gutters might leak. They eventually landed back in New England only a few miles from where they first settled after Pop retired.

This location suited Pop just fine. He spent time with his brother playing golf, worked at a local hotel as a gardener, and visited old friends. Mom said she tried to make friends, but people there were not friendly, too snobbish and standoffish. Mom's melancholy once again reared its ugly head.

I got another frantic phone call from my father.

"Peter, something is very wrong with your mother," he announced as soon as I answered the phone. "I can't take it anymore."

"What is it you can't take?" I asked. I knew from experience this question would open a litany of concerns.

"She's just not right," was all he could tell me. He then added, "You need to do something about her." His voice was a whisper as if she was nearby and he didn't want her to hear. He sounded as fully anxious and fearful as I had ever experienced from him.

Within an hour I arrived at their home. Mom was lying on the living room couch. I attempted to engage her in conversation.

"Mom, are you having any problems?" I asked her.

She mumbled incoherently. Her conversation was nonsensical. She talked about food she didn't want, places she hadn't been to, complaints about Pop, and airplanes.

"What are you talking about Mom?" I asked

"Nothing you would know anything about," she told me. She waved her hands in the air as she mumbled about planes flying around the room.

"There goes one now," she said pointing in the air. "Your father thinks I'm a robot. Maybe I am."

Mom was either playing nonsensical games with me or something in her mind had snapped. Intermittently she would get off the couch, wander into the kitchen, place a pot of water on the stove, turn the stove on, and then return to the couch. She appeared oblivious to what she had just done.

"Mom, why are you boiling water?" I asked.

"I don't know what you are talking about," she replied.

Any attempt to suggest that her actions were irrational met with a reaction from Mom.

"I don't know what the hell you are talking about," she said.

Hospital admittance loomed as a possible and obvious option. This was not her first commitment. We'd been down that road before, but her present state of resistance meant an involuntary commitment. Mom was livid at the suggestion.

"There is nothing wrong with me," she insisted. You're the crazy ones."

Involuntary commitment meant courtroom testimony. I had to hire a lawyer on Mom's behalf. It took two of us to force her into the car the day of the hearing. She adamantly refused cooperation. Her outburst in the courtroom brought the proceedings to a halt more than once. She yelled at Pop and accused me of being a "Judas". The judge granted an involuntary commitment against Mom's will.

Six months in a state mental hospital and Mom was ready to return home again. Time for another move. The big house in New England was traded for the trailer in the hills of North Carolina.

· · · ·

After five years of living in the trailer in North Carolina, my concern that they might burn down their trailer with them inside demanded that I encourage them to move once again, this time to Texas where I was living. They needed supervision. They didn't recognize this, but I did. I was particularly concerned about Mom's ongoing mental instability. I had been down this road with her too many times in the past to ignore this possibility.

Until this time, each move they made was precipitated by a set of circumstances they hoped to eliminate. Pop's anxiety over things he could not control got the best of him. Mom's loneliness and depression led to excessive drinking and mental instability. The solution was always to seek another place to live; a new location would resolve outstanding issues and provide a new lease on life. This never proved to be the case. The trailer in North Carolina was the latest in this series of moves, but safety concerns made this location impossible to sustain. I couldn't stand the thought of their being burned alive.

The day after I returned from my visit to North Carolina, I contacted a nursing home facility in the same town where I lived. I thought it an excellent choice. It was run by my church and consisted of a large campus - like facility resembling a small college. In addition to the standard nursing home services, there were condominiums, an apartment complex administered under the government Section 8 Program, and individual rooms for ambulatory residents who needed only minimal assistance. I checked out the care plans and the costs. They were favorable and affordable. I contracted for a two bedroom apartment on the first floor of the Section 8 housing complex. It had as much room as their trailer plus call buttons in case of emergency, availability of noon time meals, and twenty-four hour monitoring.

"Can we smoke? Mom asked.

"Yes. There are no restrictions on smoking, but you have to be careful where you leave your butts," I told them. Irresponsible smoking perpetuated the move out of the trailer. I didn't want a repeat performance.

"Does it have separate bedrooms?" Mom asked.

"Yes, two separate bedrooms, a full kitchen and a small dining room. Pop can park the car right out back." Another move was in the making; it was just a matter of time.

My parents, Mom and Pop, had lived together for sixty years. I urged them to consider one more move. Of course they had rigid conditions.

"Only if we can smoke there and it has separate bedrooms," they reiterated.

"You know we can't sleep in the same room," Mom added. "You father snores."

"Yes," I assured them. "The place has two bedrooms."

With that assurance they said they would think it over and get back to me. I knew that was just a stalling tactic or, at the very least, a way of letting me know they were still in charge.

Within a month, they were comfortably into their new home. All their belongings, including the car, were transported to Texas. I was given an ultimatum. "Since it was your idea we move to Texas Peter, then it's your responsibility to make sure things work out for us."

I didn't expect that kind of threat since I felt I was only assisting them make better and safer living arrangements. They saw the move as acquiescing, the first step toward relinquishing all responsibility and all blame to me if the move didn't work out. I accepted their conditions.

Separate bedrooms had always been a symbol of their relationship. It characterized the distinct and peculiar tension that existed between them. Separate bedrooms served as a safety valve. When life styles or personalities clashed, each would seek solace and comfort knowing they could retreat to their separate bedrooms.

Growing up in their household, I often felt the signs of the frustration, heard the sarcasm, witnessed the brooding, and experienced the withdrawal that characterized their personalities and the root of the tensions. This was especially evident when Mom feigned sickness or drank excessively. Pop had little tolerance for any behavior of Mom's that veered from the routine. The signs of exasperation were quite clear. A long melancholy sigh, a swear word muttered under the breath, the silent treatment were all indications of frustration between them.

At an early age I became very susceptible to the tension that existed between them. I felt particularly uneasy when I thought that the tension might lead to dissolution of the family. I imagined being without a mother or a father, a thought that created great anxiety in me. I didn't want to be orphaned. This anxiety became a source of my personal need to want to "fix" things in relationships, my fear of all that might be disruptive or divisive in family dynamics. This anxiety characterized the relationship I had with my parents and eventually transferred to other adult relationships I developed over the years. Anxiety, the fear of failure, was the overwhelming feeling I had each time I entered into a problem solving situation with Mom and Pop.

Now that Mom and Pop were in the autumn of their lives, and living under safer and more comfortable circumstances in Texas, I expected a mellowing in their relationship, that the tension that characterized their lives together might lessen considerably, and they could enter into that "peaceable kingdom" they so dreamed of upon retiring. It was not to happen.

* * * *

Photographs don't lie. They don't tell the whole truth either. Photos depict surface appearances only; an estimate of the height and weight of a person, what kind of smile they project, their gender in most cases, and maybe a hint of their age. These are facades, superficial veneers, and outward manifestations of a person. They are one dimensional. Photos reveal what a person may look like, but not what a person may be like. The single photo reveals little about the complex personality or character of a person.

Our old family photographs were misleading. One of the pictures I was drawn to was of my father walking on his hands along a boardwalk at Fire Island Beach. It is a picture of confidence. I could see the muscles in his arms straining, the smile of assurance on his face, the confidence in his body. He appeared as a man full of vibrancy and energy as if a character straight out of a novel by F. Scott Fitzgerald.

In a second photo taken about the same time, I saw my mother posing in a bathing suit on the beach. She is surrounded by smiling and adoring faces of friends looking equally attractive and confident.

Both my parents looked robust and resonant, content with life as if assured of a grand and glorious future. I was captivated by these old photographs, but also confused. The impression of my parents from these pictures bore little resemblance to the two people I now knew. I wondered what happened along life's pathways throughout the ages and stages of their youth that transformed these two people from vibrant, enthusiastic, and hopeful into disappointed, frustrated adults filled with unresolved hostility and unmet expectations. Such a conversion doesn't happen overnight. A variety of diverse forces and life changing experiences must have come into play along the way. What confused me most was that I could not pinpoint what these forces were. Aging itself seemed not to be the primary cause, but I am sure it contributed significantly.

I soon came to realize that their mental attitudes were not recent phenomenon, didn't happen overnight. They were nurtured over a long period of time. Their past experiences with mental health institutions, living with unmet expectations, carrying hopes and dreams unrelated to reality, and the attack upon their physical well being from diet, alcohol, smoking, and lack of exercise all took their toll both physically and emotionally. When I inherited them as residents of Texas, they were but a shadow of their former selves. Any comparison of pictures, now and then, would show great disparity. Despite my hopes for them of a life filled with contentment and satisfaction, the next decade would prove to be a time of great turmoil in their lives.

I was a middle child. Theory maintains that middle children hold a unique position in the family dynamics. Dr. Alfred Adler first directed our attention to certain characteristics or qualities brought on by family birth order. He suggested that middle children avoid confrontation and tend toward being peacemakers. Middle children were people-pleasers who often end up feeling manipulated and overlooked in their efforts to comply. They often felt pressured to assume roles that their siblings were unable or unwilling to fulfill. This sometimes left the middle child with a chip on his shoulder.

Middle children were most likely to become the "family caretakers", a role they intentionally assumed even if not expected of them. I assumed those traits and coveted these characteristic as if they were my birth right. Growing up in our home provided a Petri dish for the nurturing of these characteristics, an attitude I carried with me into adult hood. It was destined that I would become the parent to my parents.

When I was growing up, my parents were an enigma to me. I never fully understood what pleased them. As a consequence, intimacy between us suffered. I did not share secrets with them. I did not ask for their advice. I did not cry in their presence. I avoided like the plague any expression of feelings for fear of exposing weakness or vulnerability. I was less afraid of my own feelings and most fearful of upsetting them.

Two specific recollections are paramount. First was the feeling of guilt. I loved my parents, but didn't particularly like them. My distain was certainly not precipitated by any abuse issues. Rather it was that I disliked the constant tension that existed in our family relations and the ongoing fear I had that my parent's were not happy and content. They didn't show joy with each other. Only if they were joyful could I find joy. I didn't find much joy.

That I didn't like my parents was a source of constant guilt. The best I could conjure up was to show respect and to be responsible. Like the Hippocratic Oath, my intent was to cause them no grief and no reason to add to their displeasure with life. I did not want to be an excuse for their unhappiness.

I compensated for this guilt with an overwhelming desire to be a caretaker, by assuming responsibility for maintaining peace in the family and by intending to become the obedient son. Caretaking was my way of dealing with the guilt of discordant feelings.

Secondly, despite distancing myself from my parents, I needed their approval. I remember having strong feelings of being ignored and under-appreciated, consistent with being a middle child. I felt unworthy. I didn't excel at anything. I was not good in school. I received only C's while my brother got A's. That I was the fastest runner in third grade was not enough to elicit much parental approval.

From boxing to baseball, I was average. My father served as umpire at our little league games, but despite his leniency, I managed to strike out most times. I failed at guitar lessons. I did not graduate with my high school class because I flunked an English final exam. I entered college on probation after being refused by most of my college choices. The middle child is supposed to please people. I felt I had not been doing that. I felt I was not worthy of my parent's approval. Now as an adult child, I needed to change that.

When my parents moved to Texas, becoming their caretakers was my way of compensating for disappointing them. I could demonstrate to them how responsible a person I really was. I reasoned they might see my caretaking as a sign of worthiness and I could finally shake the long held feelings of guilt. I longed for "thankfulness", an appreciative word, an expression of my being the "good son".

Even though this story is about my parent's journey through the later years of their life, it is also about me, about what colored our relationship, about how that relationship got transformed into the unique alliance that it would become. It is their story but seen through my eyes, colored by my perspectives, prejudiced by my feelings, and embellished by my frame of reference.

2

Unsettled in Texas

"Successful aging is to feel satisfied and fulfilled, to be loved and loving, to have a purpose and a sense of future. It is to be excited about life, to find meaning and purpose in everyday existence, freely to pursue one's goals until the last moment." ...Koenig, Harold G., "Religion and Health in Later Life. *"Aging, Spirituality, and Religion: A Handbook,* Melvin Kimble, ed., p. 9.

Research of late has indicated that certain characteristics exist among those who claim to have aged successfully. One is never quite sure what "aging successfully" means. It might be a radically different experience for each person. Nonetheless some common attributes emerge.

People are more likely to experience successful aging when they recognize their skills and abilities and use them to optimize each day's experiences. They maintain goals and objectives for their lives. They are open to revision and willing to change when obstacles get in the way of achieving goals and objectives. People who believe they have control over their future and are not fearful of taking action to affect that future are more likely to achieve feelings of success. They are not stuck in routines but exhibit willingness to make life style changes when necessary.

A second attribute is the ability to make decisions. This does not preclude that they are totally independent, but it does suggest that these people are less likely to rely exclusively on external resources to promote internal contentment and satisfaction with life.

A third characteristic of successful aging is the willingness to accept the aging process. It's been discovered that attitude has an enormous role in how we age. When aging is associated with a declining quality of life it is more a consequence of attitude degeneration than physical deterioration. People believe that decline in function and quality of life is part and parcel of aging. Giving up and giving in to the declining process usually results from an unwillingness to discover coping mechanisms. Successful aging, however, involves the willingness to find new ways to achieve desired results, a willingness to seek other ways to contend with the changes of aging. Not everyone experiences aging in the same way. Just as there are certain common denominators among all aging people which can not be denied, so also are there very distinct characteristic unique to each personality.

Mom and Pop were now settled in Texas. No denying the reality that it would take some getting used to such as my having them so close as to be virtually neighbors and them living in a new community where they had to start life over again. We entered a new phase in our relationship. Expectations on both our parts were a crap shoot. We were never sure what would happen next.

With some assistance from me, life in their new two bedroom apartment took on some semblance of routine. They set up housekeeping. Pop's Chevy Malibu was parked just outside his first floor apartment. He took control of the shopping. He found the local food market and beer store on his own. He made friends with the staff and had a newspaper delivered to his door each morning. With Pop's routine beginning to take shape, life in his new digs took on an air of normalcy.

Life developed differently for Mom. Old patterns of attitude and behavior began to emerge. She found the sofa more enticing than making new friends. She spent too much time inside her home. She soon grew remorseful, complaining of not feeling well. With the exception of the few times I invited both of them to my house for an afternoon or for an occasional Sunday afternoon drive, rarely did she leave the apartment.

Despite Pop's morphing into a routine, I began to notice certain tendencies emerge in his personality. I noticed a loss of interest in activities that used to consume much of his time and talent. This was the first time that he did not have his own place with a yard in which to putter or the opportunity to repaint the interior, both of which were first priorities in previous retirement locations. He replaced gardening with television watching. He lost interest in afternoon adventures in the car and substituted reading. His activity level greatly diminished.

My father approached getting older quite differently than did my mother. Pop, to the best of my knowledge, did not suffer from dementia. He maintained a semblance of rational thinking throughout his life time. That does not mean he was mentally stable, rather that his mindset was beset by a different condition – extreme anxiety and general discontent.

Although difficult to predict accurately, successful aging is also dependent on some common emotional characteristics. The quality of life one enjoys in later life is directly related to the degree that person has maintained a healthy emotional life style. It has been noted that people who believe they control the choices they make can affect their satisfaction with old age. Rather than lament the fact of aging, they are more likely to accept it and make the best through coping mechanisms. Lacking many of the characteristics mentioned previously for successful aging, Pop succumbed to a different set of circumstances that affected his peace, his joy, his contentment in old age.

Pop suffered from disillusionment. His hopes and dreams for retirement never materialized. Beginning with his idyllic illusions of retirement – the dream of a house in the country with a worry free life style of leisure activities - his illusion remained exactly that, a self-deception, without reality, and largely unfulfilled. Despite his constant search for the idyllic retirement setting, Pop never tried to make the best of his circumstances. Life was never quite what he expected and he refused to accept the situation before him. He longed for something better, but lacked the inspiration and fortitude to achieve that goal. Someone or something outside his control was always blamed for his lack of success.

Coping was not a personality trait Pop nurtured. Routines became so important to Pop that they controlled his life. When aging demanded that he seek other ways to accomplish his goals, he was unwilling to change his life style. He maintained an attitude that if he could no longer do something the way he had always done it, he would not do it any more.

Pop made no effort to connect with his spiritual resources. I never knew him to look inward for initiative and strength. Instead he depended upon external circumstances to provide for his contentment, satisfaction, and peace. When these external resources were lacking, unfulfilled, or unrealistic, he lost his sense of hopefulness.

My father's approach to the aging process was probably not unique. Many others, I suspect, have also experienced the same feelings and attitudes as a result of the realization that their existence was not immortal. Only as an afterthought have I come to observe how his behaviors, his attitudes, and his reactions to the circumstances surrounding his later life have affected his emotional stability and physical well being during those last few years.

Mom and Pop had established a routine in the assisted living facility, but life was anything but settled.

Pop had subtle ways of demanding my attention. He could be very deceptive. Only afterward would I discover his ploy. I don't think his deception was intentional. Rather it had become his patterned way of relating to those upon whom he had become dependent. Anxiety drove his motivation. Pop was a worrier and manipulation was a way of reducing his anxiety level.

When Pop sent out his desperate calls for help, he often used my mother as his excuse.

"It's about your mother," he would say as soon as I answered the phone. The clue that I was to be confronted by a problem was his use of the words, "your mother." By referring to her as "my mother" was a clear indication that the problem was my responsibility.

A tirade of complaints followed.

"She always pretends to be sick," he would tell me. "She's a hypochondriac. She pretends to be sick just to annoy me. She drinks too much and smokes too much and I can't tell her otherwise because she gets bitcy at me." Pop always feared Mom's fits of temper. He complained that she naps all day, refused to do housework, and her moods changed as often as traffic lights, but he would not address these concerns directly with her.

Pop thrived on the routine. Mom was unpredictable. These two life perspectives were as incompatible as oil and water. Pop spent enormous energy, both physically and mentally, trying to train Mom to respect his routines; to live what he considered a "normal" life, but usually to no avail. The two personalities collided more often as they grew older together. Their tolerance of each others foibles were stretched to the limit. These collisions prompted Pop's calls of desperation to me.

"I Can't Take It Anymore"

"Peter, this is Pop." His voice sounded stressful. He was barely audible. He was calling me from a phone outside the apartment or in the hall of the nursing home in order to avoid eavesdropping on his conversation, especially by Mom.

"What's up, Pop?" I would answer. "What do you need?" I anticipated a need, not a pleasant conversation. He rarely called unless there was a problem.

"It's your mother," he told me. How many times I had heard that the previous decade. Whenever he used the term, "your mother", it meant that he was absolving himself of his responsibility for her and transferring it to me. "I can't take it anymore."

"What's the problem?" I asked. I sounded surprised and feigned innocence of any hint that I might have imagined he would have a problem with Mom.

"Everything, "he said. "I can't take it anymore."

"What can't you take? "I asked. I felt a pang of exasperation suddenly overcome me and reacted with a bit of sarcasm. I knew full well he was about to unleash a litany of complains and faults about Mom.

"Your mother. She's driving me crazy. The woman is not normal." Pop had an altered perception of normal. Normal was whatever met his present expectations.

"I don't know what you mean, Pop. What is she doing that is so bad?" I tried to coax him to focus on specifics rather than the usual vague and ambiguous innuendos. I encouraged him to pinpoint some particular behaviors that might be remedied or resolved, but I got no help from him.

"She's just not normal," he kept repeating. "You know what I mean. You know how she acts. You've got to do something. I just can't take it anymore." I noticed he referred to "it" rather than mother. When he said "I just can't take *it* any more," I realized it wasn't mother that was the real source of his discontentment. She was merely the scapegoat. Pop's exasperation was with life in general and old age in particular.

"Well, I'll see what I can do," I told him. It was less a promise and more a put-off, a diversion, a stalling technique. I had gained much practice stalling over the past few years.

Pop let his pent up frustrations explode without provocation. I had always maintained that letting go of feelings was better than denying them or burying them deep inside. Pop, however, seemed to "let go" too frequently. His inability to identify particulars only reinforced my hunch that his beef wasn't with Mom or the assisted living facility staff or me, but a result of his own inner discontent. Mom was his scapegoat, a convenient outlet for inner disappointment and disillusionment. Pop was unable to recognize the source of his displeasure.

"I'll see what I can do," I repeated. I told him I had to go and hung up.

I didn't know what I could do. I did recognize that Pop's discontent was not Mom. She might aggravate the problem or sometimes become the catalyst, but she wasn't the cause. He was just an unhappy camper. His interpretation of "normal" varied so wildly that his expectations exceeded any hope of compliance.

Pop's total and complete reliance on routines added to his discontent. Routines were not always controllable and when Pop felt out of control he felt out of sorts. Mom happened to be the closest person and most vulnerable and took the brunt of his exasperation. When his inner frustrations reached the boiling point, he called me.

"Peter, I can't take it anymore."

Pop was his own worst enemy and the source of his own discontent. He constantly struggled with anxiety, the kind that comes with a fear of the future and fretting over that which he has no control. He wished he could change that which he was not able to and refused to change that which he was able to change. He lived in a kind of limbo that comes with the feeling that one's expectation are always being thwarted by others and goals hung just at the end of one's fingers but still far enough away not to be grasped securely. His anxiety rendered him immobile much of the time.

Pop never achieved relief from his discontent with life. He allowed his external environment to be the measuring rod of his contentment. Inner peace eluded him precisely because he allowed external conditions to determine his inner satisfaction and well being. Mom's temperament was external to Pop but he adamantly refused to accept her as she was and wished for her to be as he expected. To the day he died, his hopefulness remained futile.

The content of spirituality is the ability to find wholeness and meaning in life no matter what the circumstances, the age or stage of life, or the particular situation. Spirituality recognizes that we need to keep all problems, all fears in perspective; we are human beings and as such, are imperfect, prone to error, and not always strong enough to change. If Pop could have recognized that aspect of his own nature, he might have been more accepting of and less agitated by Mom.

External conditions and expectations of what might be colored Pop's perspective on life. With little or no control of the external and unrealistic expectations of other people, Pop was left with a temperament of discontent that served only to make his days and nights miserable.

On those occasions meant specifically for reflection of life and celebration of good times and circumstances, Pop was never one to revel. Instead these occasions seemed to be more a source of annoyance than a reason for celebration.

Fading Memories

Memories are not too reliable. For instance, we can easily remember the pleasant past, but blot out the unpleasant. Nothing unusual there.

Each time Mom and Pop moved, despite being for the best of intentions, they remember the move as the worst of experiences. What they tended to forget was how dissatisfied and discontent they were where they previously lived and the reasons instigating the move. It was too cold, too isolated, to difficult to get around, too many mechanical failures, and unfriendly people. Instead they inevitably claimed that they never should have moved because life was so much more pleasant back there. Once the move was made, however, recollections of these bad experiences were soon forgotten and regrets were many about having to make the move.

"We never should have moved here," Pop was anxious to tell anyone who would listen. "We were quite comfortable where we were."

"But Pop don't you remember how miserable you said you were living back there?" I reminded him.

"What are you talking about," he said. "I loved it back there."

No amount of coaxing could convince Pop to remember how much he disliked his previous address. Once he made a change, he thought it always a bad one.

My parents' history during the last decade is evidence of their constant discontent with their home place. When they lived in Vermont, Pop's idyllic retirement home, they hated the weather. Ice buildup under the shingles and the furnace made funny noises, omens of disaster to come. They moved to Florida. Too much rain and leaves in the gutters that threatened to cause leaks increased Pop's anxiety and he wished he were back in Vermont where everything was perfect. Maine was their next location where they encountered house problems and cold damp weather which served to remind him how blissful and bucolic Florida had been.

Living in the trailer in North Carolina was meant to meet all Pop's expectations, cool in summer, warm in winter, easy maintenance, low cost, and a friendly environment. When the maintenance problems built up, he fondly remembered how Idyllic life had been in Vermont or Florida or Maine. He neglected to remember that he was years younger at those times and even then, those places presented him with overwhelming troubles.

The apartment at Eden Home was maintenance free. Noon meals were provided as an option. Staff was available for assistance when needed. Each apartment was equipped for the handicapped. An emergency pull cord was available in the bathroom. It was a first floor, two bedroom apartment. He parked his car outside his door.

"There is nothing for me to do here," Pop complained. Mom liked doing nothing so I didn't hear her grievances.

"Why don't you eat lunch in the dining hall so you can get to know other residents?" I suggested. Mom liked that idea since she hated cooking.

"Why should I get to know them?" Pop said. "They need to get to know me first. I wish we had never left our trailer in North Carolina. Life was good there. Why did you make us move?"

I can understand how difficult it must be to acknowledge that what he now had was better than what he once had, particularly when it wasn't his idea to change. Moving to Texas was my idea, I was responsible, and I was to blame for any dissatisfaction they experienced. Holding on to the past, despite its difficulties and disappointments, remains important to the person who recognizes that life is slowly slipping away. Part of the struggle of growing older is the realization that the past holds better memories than the present and the acceptance that the future holds dim prospects.

Visiting the Garden

I have inherited many traits from Pop. I am most like him when I am in my garden. Whenever Pop would visit at my house, it was our habit to take a walk out back to look at my garden. Walks were limited and slow due to the increased pain he said he was feeling in his legs.

Neither of us were experts at gardening. I do take pride and pleasure in some simple outdoor activities inherited from Pop such as mowing the grass, planting new trees and bushes, digging in freshly turned dirt to find worms, and growing radishes and tomatoes. If nothing else flourished in Pop's garden, he was content if the tomatoes and radishes turned out well. I had planted tomatoes and radishes in my garden.

This particular day I wanted to show Pop the small sprouts of radishes just emerging from the ground and the seedling tomatoes I had just planted. I was proud of them and hoped he would appreciate the similarity of my garden to the many he had planted over his many years. I hoped he would feel a sense of pride in passing on a tradition successfully. I assumed that happiness for Pop was associated with fond recollections. Besides I was looking for a way to spawn some conversation. It was a diversionary technique I used as rudimentary therapy. He had seemed despondent over the past few weeks.

"Well what do you think of my radishes and tomatoes," I asked him? I thought it was a better start to hopeful conversation than the usual "how are you feeling."

"The tomatoes seem to be taking off well," I told him. "I pinched off some of the sucker shoots already. Remember that's what you taught me. That ought to make them bloom better don't you think?"

Pop looked thoughtful for a moment. He didn't say anything. I watched his face. He didn't look interested. He had a rather blank look.

"Now you need to give them a little side dressing with fertilizer and scratch it into the soil," he eventually responded.

That sounded like a good start to a conversation, I thought, as well as good gardening advice.

"I can do that right now," I told him. I started for the backyard shed where I kept my bag of 15-10-10 fertilizer. "Let me get my wheelbarrow," I called back to him. "Then I need you to show me how much to put on." Pop sat on the bench by the garden.

"Okay," he said as I headed toward the shed.

As I was scooping the fertilizer out of the bag and into a pot in the wheelbarrow to carry back to the garden, I heard Pop call out to me, "Peter, I'm going inside." It was an unplanned, abrupt departure. Something was amiss. I knew it and so did Pop. I let him go without comment.

I left the fertilizer in the wheelbarrow and followed Pop inside. "Is something wrong, "I asked him?

At first he responded, "No, nothing is wrong." Shortly afterwards, however, he added, "I don't want to see gardens anymore, Peter. They bring up sad memories."

"What sad memories," I asked him? "I thought you always liked gardens. I thought you loved to work in them."

"I do," he answered. "At least I did. But I can't do gardening anymore. I can't bend down and it hurts to lift things."

"You know we can always find a way to get around those problems if you still want to work that small patch behind the nursing home," I said. "The staff said they would help you as much as they can. They can do the heavy stuff and I can carry and dig for you. They need someone to keep the flowers going."

I expected some reluctance. Pop always said "no" when first asked to do something new. Usually after some time to think and hear some convincing conversation, he would agree to at least try it.

"If you need some special tools or maybe a bench to sit on, we can get those things easily," I reassured him. "I just want you to be able to do the things you always liked to do."

"If I can't do gardening like I used to do it then I don't want to do it at all," he told me. "Sitting on a bench isn't the way to do good gardening. I just don't want to do that." He had an air of resignation in his voice.

Pop was having great difficulty compensating. He knew he was growing older and he realized that he couldn't do his favorite activities in the same way he was used to doing them. He needed a cane to walk because his legs hurt. He could only drive during the day because of failing eyesight. Even his beer consumption had to be curtailed because of his limited capacity to hold urine. Many activities he used to take for granted, those done with ease with hardly a second thought, now became challenges.

Pop resisted challenges, unless he was willing to compensate. He had to find ways of accomplishing those tasks differently. He chose not to do this. His stubbornness won out and took control. Compensating was not an option. If he was not able to do something the way he had always done it, then he wouldn't do it at all. He focused his memories on the way things used to be. But recollections of good times were becoming painful. Those memories reminded him of how things once were and were no longer. Pop didn't seem able to grow old gracefully. He fought it the whole way. He felt desperation knowing that his time was slipping away. In his mind he wanted to remain as he always was and then die.

I hesitated to include Pop in any activities I was doing if they hinted at something he used to like. I was afraid he would become even more deeply saddened and depressed. Memories, instead of being fond, often bring out frustrations and a certain melancholy, a relinquishing spirit that can easily overcome a person with doldrums. Spiritual care is sensitive to what is breaking into life, changing life, renewing life, but not returning life to the way it always has been. I was never able to convince Pop that life as it used to be was not an option and to focus on this perspective only brings disappointment.

The Malibu

When Mom and Pop moved to Texas, they brought with them their 1982 Chevrolet Malibu. It was huge, with four doors and an eight cylinder engine under the hood. Fins protruded from the rear and extra large tires came as standard equipment. Pop bought it used from a rental car company. He said he got a good deal. It had low mileage and he was told it had only been driven on the freeways.

Pop was a stickler for safety. The Malibu, he maintained, was one of the safest cars on the road because it was well built. It averaged about twelve miles per gallon of gas. The price of gas was not a concern for him since he drove it only around town.

Pop took good care of the Malibu. He parked it carefully outside his apartment near a window so he could watch if anyone parked too close. He had the oil changed every three months or three hundred miles, whichever came first. He used the car only when necessary, going to the grocery store, to the beer store, and to the drug store. Occasionally he drove it to visit at my house.

Pop said Mom didn't want to drive anymore. Mom said Pop wouldn't let her drive. I was allowed to drive on Sunday afternoons when I took them exploring in the countryside or acclimating them to their new community.

Pop had the annoying habit of checking his watch frequently.

"It's nearly four o'clock, Peter," he reminded me. "I need to be home by five."

He reminded me of the same situation every fifteen minutes. Pop's routine demanded he have supper completed on Sunday before the *60 Minutes* television show came on. His routine was unchangeable.

My father was reminded of his prostate cancer by the pains he had in his legs periodically. After we returned home one Sunday afternoon he reminded me also.

"My legs hurt too much to drive anymore," he told me.

"Your car is an automatic," I reminded him. "You hardly use your legs except to get in and out."

"I can't see any good," he added.

"You remember the doctor said there is nothing wrong with your eyesight so long as you wear your glasses," I told him. "You don't want to stop driving, do you?" I asked.

"I don't need to go anywhere," he said.

"Then how come you call me every other day to take you somewhere to get something you say you need right away," I said. "If you drove yourself, you could go when you wanted to." I'm sure my voice sounded a bit agitated.

I interpreted his reluctance to drive as a sign of his waning independence. I thought it unrelated to his ability and more an indication of his growing resignation. I was concerned that without a strong feeling for remaining independent, his resolve toward self-reliance about all matters would quickly wane. I wanted him to remain an autonomous person as long as possible, thus relieving me of additional responsibilities. A selfish thought, but honest nonetheless.

"Pop, you need to drive yourself," I encouraged him. "What's the problem with driving? You've been doing it for sixty years with no problem."

"I just don't want to drive anymore," he insisted. "I get too nervous."

I tried to compromise. "Tell you what," I said. "I'll drive you where you want to go if you'll drive the Malibu over to my house to pick me up." There was no indication that his driving had become dangerous. My reasoning was that if he decided to drive to my house, a distance of ten miles, he would realize that it was far more convenient to drive to the store himself. I was wrong.

"If you don't want to drive me, then you might as well take the car because I'm not driving anymore," he told me much to my chagrin.

I took the Malibu to my house and parked it in the street. I wondered and worried about the consequences. Was this the end of Pop's independence? Was I now becoming solely responsible for his transportation needs? Was giving up this aspect of his independence an omen that soon all his independence would be sacrificed?

We never talked about the Malibu again. It sat in front of my house unused for months. When Pop came for a visit, he would walk past the car as if he never noticed it. He didn't ask whether I changed the oil regularly or if I fixed the leak in the trunk. I thought he might ask to drive the Malibu again when I took him for rides on Sunday afternoons. He never did. It was as if he never owned the car.

The Malibu sat unused at my house almost a year before I ventured to drive it. Each time I looked at it, I was reminded that it was the last vestige of Pop's independence, a thought that brought sadness in my heart.

Mental Health Concerns

Having lived in the apartment now for almost a year, I noticed drastic changes in the attitudes of both my parents. Since moving, Pop never regained much interest in activities he used to like and rebuffed my suggestions for participating in any of the activities offered through the assisted living facility.

Mom started acting seriously lethargic. She complained about chronic stomach cramps.

"Nobody should have to suffer like this," Mom exclaimed the minute I entered their apartment. "Night times are the worse. That's why I have to take naps during the day."

Most days she fell asleep on the couch while reading a book or watching television. Later she would awake, make her way to the bedroom, but complain she couldn't fall asleep again. A pattern was formed. She slept during the day but not at night. Whenever confronted about this reversal of routines, she made sure that Pop and I knew of her ailments and paid proper respect to her condition.

"No one should suffer like I have to," she repeated.

"How about we take a walk together?" I suggested.

"I can't walk with these pains," she responded. The look on her face clearly showed indignation.

Frequent visits to the doctor only exasperated the situation. Tests found no sign of intestinal problems, no cancer, and no symptoms of any other ailment. The doctor suggested some remedies – change her diet, stay awake longer during the day, pursue a hobby – but each was rejected as "silly" by Mom. When the doctor suggested walking, she blew off his advice as that of a quack. What she resented most was that someone besides herself might know what was good for her.

"You have no idea what you are talking about," she repeated. "You don't know how sick I am. Stop telling me what I ought to do." She repeated this to me, my father, the doctors, and anyone else who offered advice.

Mom had gone through moods of depression and agitation previously, but this time they seemed to linger longer and settle in more deeply. She appeared to be losing her rational thought, losing her ability to take care of herself, and cutting herself off from all relationships. She became argumentative. I was afraid she was becoming a danger to herself. She refused to act on her own behalf. Thoughts of mental instability once again surfaced. We had been down this road so many times.

Pop's reaction was predictable. He became exasperated with her and easily lost his temper when she continued to verbally assault him. Life with Mom began to feel like a "B" movie, something from a science fiction or horror script. Both Mom and Pop teetered on the edge of a mental breakdown. I suggested counseling, but Mom laughed and continued to maintain that perhaps I was the one needing counseling. I broached the subject again a few days later.

"Okay." Mom said.

"What do you mean, Okay?" I asked.

"I mean okay. I'll do what you suggest. I'll go to a hospital," Mom replied.

Awestruck, I wasted no time in consulting with a doctor for Mom to have an observation period, a brief intake period as a patient in a psychiatric hospital.

The next day, I got a call from Pop.

"Peter, I want to go with Mom," he said.

"Sure. You can ride with me and I'll bring you back after she's admitted," I told him.

"No. I mean I want to stay with her at the hospital," he said.

Considering Pop's extreme agitation and anxiety, I offered no resistance. I told him I would talk with the doctor to see if that could happen. The doctor assured me it could happen. Apparently any paying patient was always welcomed.

They were both checked into the adult unit, a locked unit, with fewer complications than checking into a Holiday Inn.

"Can we smoke here?" was the only question they had when asked by the admitting staff if they had any concerns. When told they could smoke in supervised areas, they were placated. They each had a private room without a bath.

They were confined to the unit except for supervised dining hall privileges. Individual and group therapy occupied part of each day, arts and crafts consumed more time. Pop refused the arts projects claiming they were childish. They watched television in the day room. Occasionally they argued with other residents about channels and volume. Pop read magazines and Mom read books. I wondered about the activities; that they were the same ones they did at home that led to their mental demise.

"Oh but they are making good progress," I was reassured by the counselors.

Whenever I visited I encountered a litany of complaints. The books in the library were terrible, I needed to bring more. They made Mom eat too fast and it upset her stomach. Pop couldn't watch Sixty Minutes on Sunday evenings because there were too many visitors. Both never had enough cigarettes. Other than these minor annoyances, I was surprised they registered few complaints about being locked into a psychiatric hospital. The loss of freedom caused them little concern.

The insurance was soon to run out. Mom and Pop were scheduled for "out take interviews". I was asked to be present as the staff talked with them about plans for the future. No specific diagnosis was conclusive, no medication prescribed, and no referrals were noted.

"Where do you want to live after being discharged?" they asked both of them.

"I don't care," they responded in unison.

"Do you want to go back to your apartment?

Again they responded, "I don't care."

"Do you think you can take care of yourselves?" a staff person asked.

"I don't know," each stated.

"Well what do you want to do now?

"I don't know," was their response again.

I was aghast. Were they expecting me to make a decision for them? They couldn't stay at the hospital. Insurance payments expired. There was no compelling diagnosis to keep them there. They expressed no desire to go home. I was in a quandary. I had to make a decision for them, but if it proved wrong, I was responsible. I was left with no choice.

"If you don't know what you want to do or where you want to live and if you can't take care of yourselves, then you will have to live in the nursing home," I told them.

"I don't care," they each responded.

I never wanted to totally usurp their personal responsibility, but the lack of response forced the issue. I felt like a parent making decisions for small children. It didn't feel right, but had to be done since neither of them was forthcoming.

We went straight from the hospital to the nursing home. When the nursing home staff asked me what the prevailing circumstances that precipitated the move were, I responded, "We ran out of options."

"Can we smoke here?" was the first question the asked the admittance person. "And we need separate rooms."

3

Unholy Life in the Nursing Home

"In a hospital they throw you out into the streets before you are half cured, but in a nursing home they don't let you out till you are dead."...George Bernard Shaw

I was advised by fiends that keeping parents in their own homes even under the worst of conditions was always better than putting them in a nursing home. Confining parents to a nursing home, they maintained, was nothing less than parental abuse. Maybe so, maybe not.

"I could never put my mother in a nursing home. It seems so cruel." Nursing homes, some claim, are uncaring, neglectful institutions that prey on vulnerable, feeble, and senile old people. The staff is untrained, the care is minimal, and the real concern is profit. "Besides, Mom is not ready and I promised her I would never send her to a nursing home."

These words uttered with such empathy often come back to haunt the speaker. It's a possibility that mother may prefer the security and independence of a modern assisted living facility rather than the self imposed prison of her own home.

Perhaps grandma hints that she would rather stay in her own home as long as possible. You concur. But what does "as long as possible" mean? After a short period of providing medical assistance, cleaning up after incontinence, managing two homesteads, parental bathing, shopping for two families, and a great deal of worrying and wondering if you have done it all correctly, you learn that, despite your best efforts, grandma doesn't approve of how you handled affairs. Constant complaints coupled with sheer exhaustion leads to feelings of being unappreciated. Resentments set in. The caring and loving relationship between parent and adult child evaporates and is soon replaced by antagonism, spite, and hostility. Broken promises and unmet expectations have taken their toll.

Moving grandma into your own house sounded like a reasonable resolution to a major concern and a way to renew a relationship. Grandma gets to listen to the heavy metal music of the teenaged granddaughter, the fits of temper of the autistic son, and the incessant barking of Fido the dog. The one bathroom down the hall is constantly in use and grandma is the last to reach it. You want grandma to feel wanted and appreciated; to know that she is an important part of the family structure. Generational nurture is important to you. It doesn't always end up they way it is envisioned.

Elderly adults can be very demanding and show little gratitude. It is not unusual for the caretakers to begin to harbor ill will and malice toward the aging parents. Such feelings are not what were intended when the decision was made to take care of grandma in your home.

Assisted living facilities and skilled care homes can assist in rejuvenating family relationships rather than decimating them. Freed from the sole responsibility of meeting all the needs of an aging parent or grandparent allows for the energy needed for rebuilding and renewing relationships. Gone are the feelings of being unduly burdened. Feeling unappreciated is not an issue. Parents don't blame you for all problems. You are not responsible for meeting all your parent's expectations. Feelings of inadequacy are removed. You may have to work on the guilt for a while.

Living alone in one's own house during advanced age is not always independent living. Constant worries about daily household tasks – leaky plumbing, yard work, paying bills on time, stopped up toilets – and the threat of sickness or accident can make independent living feel more like imprisonment. Assisted living or skilled care living for grandma can offer "freedom" from this imprisonment.

Spend time building or rebuilding relationships rather than changing adult diapers or monitoring medications or cleaning a bathroom. When grandma lived at her own home or your home there never seemed to be enough time or energy to just sit and listen or have a conversation about past memories or watch television while grandma knitted. You were too busy with bottom line necessities like cooking, cleaning, meeting doctors appointments, and other necessities. When living in an assisted facility, you and grandma can spend time on conversation about family matters, about old and good times together, about experiences you still have left to accomplish on your bucket lists.

The fear of assisted living or nursing homes is more imagined than real. Sometimes we make poor choices, but that is not indicative of all homes. When put under close scrutiny for what matters for the elderly, nursing homes score fairly well. Repairing a bond between aging parents and an adult child goes a long way towards healthy relationship that matter and building lasting memories that both you and your parent take to your graves.

When my parents became my neighbors, I realized that a once a week telephone call to check up on their circumstances no longer would be sufficient. I could not renege on the responsibility of visiting with them since they lived so close by. When they moved to the assisted living facility, they retained some mobility, did most of their own shopping and visited at my house as the mood served them. The necessity of scheduled regular visitation seemed less a necessity.

In the nursing home, all independent travel was relinquished. If any visitation were to happen, it would be one way. I had to initiate the visits. At first these visits were unscheduled. I would drop by as frequently as I saw fit or as could be allotted by my work schedule and family obligations. This became too haphazard. I never seemed to schedule visit times suitable to both my schedule and their growing needs. If I came by unannounced they claimed they were engaged otherwise – naps, reading, meal times, scheduled baths or other such daily necessities they or the staff found important. The solution – I scheduled specific times for regular visits. I informed the staff of these times and attempted to impress on my parents the importance of these specific times as well. I asked if they could try to make themselves available at those times, uninterrupted by other activities. This schedule of visits allowed me the freedom to arrange my time so as to be both available to them regularly as well as to my other obligations without interruption. Neither of my parents necessarily conformed to my requests.

There are many "experts" who offer advice on visiting family in the nursing home. I consulted some. I include a summery of their poignant suggestions, but admit upfront that although they sound constructive and supportive, I found them generic to the point of being naïve. Every family's circumstance is different. Few common denominators exist between individuals residing in nursing homes just as they exist between unique personalities in the general public. Despite every effort I made to abide by the "tips" for visiting in the nursing home, I was constantly challenged by my parent's circumstances and unique personalities. When combined together, circumstances and personalities rarely ever conform to any standards.

In her work with The Ohio State University Department of Aging, Dr Christine A. Price suggests the following as standards for visiting in the nursing home. (Price, Christine A., *Tips When Visiting a Nursing Home, SS-188-01,*). Despite being aware of these "tips" rarely were they functional for me or my parents

• *Be supportive and affectionate.* The only times I had the opportunity to be supportive was when I attempted to respond to some arbitrary grievances Pop or Mom or both laid on me. Most times, the episodes revolved around uncontrollable, real or imaginary, concerns that had no bearing on reality. Perhaps unique to our own family dynamics, affection was not a priority. No hand holding, hugging, or eye contact was prevalent and intimacy was at a minimum.

• *Ask permission to visit and then plan your visits in advance.* "Can I come see you Thursday afternoon?" was not a question I often asked, nor was much effort given to planning for the visits. I visited according to my own schedule and, with few exceptions, I planned our time together to be as limited as I thought I could get away with without feeling overly guilty.

• *Listen attentively to your loved ones.* Since I anticipated the content of most of our conversations, attentive listening was not a skill I acquired and practiced with much acumen. What information they provided to me in these conversations was not meant as shared enjoyment but rather as fodder for remedying problems.

• *Bring your children to encourage relationship building.* My children rarely visited nor did I encourage it. They had no previous nurturing relationship with either Mom or Pop as grandparents. Frankly, there was little love lost by either party.

• *Make a point to acknowledge other residents.* The few times I said hello or struck up conversations with other residents, I was usually admonished. Other residents were an annoyance to both my parents and any contact with them was seen as competition for my time.

• *Share news about your life.* My concerns, my family, my experiences encouraged little response from Mom and Pop. Each visit they interpreted as "their time." Any alternative to addressing their concerns was an interruption. I don't remember a single query from them about how I was doing or how my family was making out.

Living Together in Separate Rooms

Eden Home nursing facility suggested separate rooms, one for Pop and another for Mom. They proved more than accommodating, assigning Mom and Pop to rooms in different sections of the facility. So confusing was the labyrinth of interconnecting hallways that I doubted that they could find each other's rooms without a GPS system.

This separation was agreed to by Pop. Mom simple acquiesced. Their insistence on separate rooms was precipitated by the snoring factor, but I knew other factors entered into the decision. Mom's dementia began to affect her behavior. Pop said that she embarrassed him when they were together in the common living room. She insisted on chain smoking and dropped ashes on the floor, she was rude to other residents, and she dressed "funny". Mom complained that Pop would not talk to her, that he purposely avoided her, and he would not share his cigarettes. She didn't say she could not find his room.

Pop did intentionally avoid Mom as often as he could. He ate at a different time and sometimes in a different dining hall to confuse her. He refused to tell her his room number. He retreated to his room immediately after each meal, sometimes sneaking down different hallways so Mom would not be able to follow him.

I scolded Pop for being so inconsiderate.

"She annoys the hell out of me and all the other people," he said. "It's embarrassing to me Peter. They think she is a loony."

When Mom's memory began to fail, Pop started to lie to her. He told her he lived in a different building, that cigarettes were not allowed at the home, and that he had to go places that didn't exist. Sometimes I would find him sitting and reading in a small, out of the way, sun room.

"Why are you way over here," I asked

"Your mother can't find me here," he told me.

Mom didn't know enough to question him. She just accepted what he told her.

Mom grew very accepting of living at the nursing home. Her developing dementia certainly aided in this acceptance. She didn't have to fix meals or do housework which suited her temperament. Her health improved drastically as she responded to regular and supervised medications. More fruits and vegetables were added to her diet. There were no complaints of a "weak colon" or stomach cramps or diarrhea.

Her confusion and lapses in memory had a calming effect on her bouts of depression. As time passed, despite my reminding her frequently, she forgot where she was living. She was unsure of family members even when I identified them by name and relationship. I shared stories and news about my brothers, cousins, and uncles and when I finished speaking, she would ask who I as talking about. Forgetting didn't upset her, it just didn't worry her.

Mom's dementia continued to build and began affecting her daily life in other ways besides memory. She had difficulty eating solid food as if she forgot how to chew. She grew easily agitated at the staff when they attempted to assist her. She became incontinent, but flatly denied it. Complete sentences were a struggle.

I never wanted to give up hope that their remaining years together would be a time of renewing their relationship, but this seemed less and less likely. I encouraged them to spent time together, but such coaxing fell on deaf ears. Only on those occasions when I took them out or invited them to my house did they spend considerable time together in the same room and converse with each other.

To everyone else – the staff at the nursing home, other residents, visitors, the rest of my family – Mom and Pop were a couple. I now knew them differently, separately, almost strangers to each other. I felt like a referee rather than a peacemaker. I felt like I needed to maintain walls that separated them rather than provide experiences that brought them together, I provided damage control after hurt feelings. I had two parents still living, but it felt less and less like a family.

Geriatric Power Struggles

There has been some discussion recently about the "exchange theory" first proposed by Dowd (Dowd, J.J., *Aging as Exchange: A preface to theory,* Journal of Gerontology, September 30, 1975, pp.584–94). In any relationship, he maintains, there exists a balance of exchange. When each person's resources are comparatively equal, a mutually satisfying interdependence may emerge. Both prosper in the relationship. Exchange relations that get too far out of balance may lead to unstable relationships with negative consequences for parties, the care giver and the care recipient. When an aging parent becomes too dependent upon the caretaker, i.e., me, the balance of give and take is out of whack. The care giver resents the intrusion and the care recipient resents the loss of independence. I could feel this dynamic happening between Pop and me.

. . . .

"Peter, is that you?" I am the only person Pop ever calls, but he sounds surprised when I answer the phone. It was eight-thirty on a Tuesday night. He was calling from the nursing home.

"Yep, it's me Pop. What's up?" I learned never to begin a conversation with Pop, on the phone or in person, with "how are you?" Even if he were feeling quite well that day, he would not admit it. "How are you?" was an invitation for a litany of long suffering.

"Peter, I can't find my cigarette lighter," he told me. "I need you to bring one up for me."

Since moving into the nursing home, the staff and I had made concerted efforts to curtail the amount of smoking for both my parents. We tried pleading – "Don't you know what smoke is doing to your insides?" We tried the guilt factor – "Smoking is very bothersome to the other residents who don't smoke." Neither Mom nor Pop seemed willing to accept changes.

The staff mandated that all lighters and matches be kept at the nursing stations. Enforcement was lax, however. Pop knew the rules, but his reluctance to live by the rules curtailed his willingness to ask for a light. The aides were often not at the nursing stations, so Pop kept a lighter in his pocket.

"I can do that," I told him. "No problem. I'll bring one up tomorrow."

Tomorrow was Wednesday. Every Wednesday and Sunday I visited the nursing home. Now that Pop refused to drive, there was usually something he wanted me to bring each time I visited – a newspaper, Tylenol night time pills, Kleenex, or some handkerchiefs. I tried to set limits on how often I would play "go fetch". Twice per week seemed reasonable. My hope was that Pop would schedule his needs for those days. Rarely did that happen.

"But I need it now, Peter, tonight." Pop didn't sound consoled. "Peter, I've got to be able to light my cigarettes." When he used my name twice in succession, it suggested a pending crisis.

"Pop, why can't you borrow a match from someone?"

It was approaching nine o'clock. I had just returned home from a meeting and was not looking forward to going out again that night. Pop's requests for deliveries were never convenient.

"Ask a staff person," I continued. "Or maybe you can get a light from Mr. Reagan. You usually smoke with him anyway. I can bring a lighter up tomorrow."

Pop didn't like Mr. Reagan. His reasoning was very parochial. Mr. Reagan was from Texas. Pop lived his life in New England. Mr. Reagan wasn't the least bit interested in what happened in New England and Pop responded with only a cursory attention to stories about Texas. It was a standoff, like two young boys arguing about whose father was stronger. They eventually tired of the conflict and ignored the subject altogether. They sat together silently in the smoking area.

"He's just not my kind," Pop would tell me when I inquired about his friend, Mr. Reagan. He didn't like President Regan and I suspect there was some transference going on. He wanted to keep the relationship alive, but only at a distance. Pop called him his "smoking accomplice." Only a few people at the home smoked. It was a mutually necessary relationship but without intimacy of friendship. Asking Mr. Reagan for a light bordered on acknowledging a friendship and Pop was not ready to do that.

"I can't do that," was his response to my suggestion that he ask Mr. Reagan for a light.

"Why not?' I asked him

"Just because I can't," seemed to be his final answer. "It won't take you but a few minutes to bring me a lighter," he added. I was sure he sensed my hesitation and reluctance. He was correct. It felt like an intrusion on my limited time. I was feeling resentful and put upon. Shame on me.

"Peter, I never ask much from you," Pop added. I sequestered his sarcasm. I thought to myself, "Yes you do."

"This is such a small favor," he continued. I sensed his manipulative powers switching into high gear. "You know, Peter, there is not much I have to live for these days. Smoking is about the only enjoyment I have, what with your mother bothering me all the time." Adding "your mother" to his litany of long suffering had become his latest habit when impressing me with the urgency of his requests. "But if you don't want me to smoke anymore, I guess I'll just have to endure that as well."

"I don't want you to stop smoking. I mean, I do, but I know you enjoy it and won't stop. You can smoke all you want to," I told him.

I was being exploited by an expert. I was losing clarity in my thoughts. He knew that dropping the slightest hint that I was unresponsive and uncaring would jolt me into action. To play on my guilt that I wasn't living up to my responsibility as a "good" son was a strong motivating factor for Pop.

"Smoke all you want," I told him. "I'm just asking you to find a light from someone up there instead of my having to go out again tonight. That's all I'm asking." I could feel my voice rising, nearing a crescendo as anger welled up inside.

Pop wasn't swayed by compassion for me. "I ask so little from you," I heard him say. "If it's too much trouble, just forget it." He hung up the phone abruptly.

We settled on a stalemate. Neither of us seemed willing to budge. I knew that Pop didn't really feel I was a neglectful and uncaring person. I hoped that by the next afternoon he would have forgotten the previous night's conversation.

It was a test of our relationship. He wanted reassurance that he wasn't abandoned and alone. He needed to know that he was still very important in my life and I would respond to his needs.

I needed some perspective on our relationship. Previously I felt I had given into non-essential requests for my time and attention. I knew there was a fine line between caring and being manipulated. I was struggling to discover the boundaries. I felt I had a right to reject the frivolous.

The spirituality of a person is often reflected in the need to be needed. For Pop, this need manifested itself in his constant search for evidence that he was important to someone else – to me. His requests, even the most frivolous, were acts in search of reassurance that I still loved him and cared about him.

For me, responding to his requests, including the occasional frivolous, were actions taken to convince myself that I was needed. It was a symbiotic relationship; we each existed to serve the needs of the other. Pop also found this need met in other relationships.

Much has been written concerning emotional blackmail. Michael Lee, author of "How To Be An Expert Persuader… In 20 Days or Less" offers some tips on avoiding emotional blackmail. First and foremost, he suggests, is to recognize the signs. Emotional blackmail is characterized by six distinct stages. (1) Demand- when a person asks you to do something for him. (2) Resistance – conveying your difficulty in honoring the request. (3) Pressure – he backs you into a corner. (4) Threats – when you are told that not giving in may have dire consequences. (5) Compliance – giving up and giving in. (6) Repetition – the cycle repeats itself.

I was dealing with my father. His requests were paramount. I constantly struggled with how to deny his requests and not feel guilty. It's like saying to yourself, yes, this is family, blood relations, people I love and care about, but so what? I have to protect myself even more.

The Smoking Habit

Smoking was pure joy to both my parents. The older they got, the more they smoked. Every waking hour was heralded as an opportunity to have another cigarette. They considered smoking as an inherent "right" of citizenship.

Despite its pleasure, it also caused them unending grief. It was a safety issue. While living in the trailer in North Carolina burn holes appeared in the furniture, ashes on the rugs, and cigarette butts in the wastebaskets. One day, while my mother snoozed on the living room couch, I watched her cigarette fall from her hands onto her sweater and immediately burn a hole before I retrieved it.

"Mom, you're dropping a lighted cigarette on your stomach," I shouted to her excitedly. I put the butt out in the ash tray.

"Oh I am not," she replied. "I don't know what you are talking about."

I had already discarded the evidence so I had nothing to show her.

I noticed that Pop would leave lighted cigarettes on table edges, sinks and counter tops, and on the back stoop. Apparently he put them down, forgot about them, and then lit another cigarette.

Trailers are notorious fire hazards. Once a fire starts, it's like being trapped in an oven. Their disregard for fire safety frightened me. Their constant smoking habit was what convinced me that the move to Texas was in order. Supervision was necessary and mandated. After moving into the apartment in Texas, they appeared more careful, but still occasionally ignored lighted butts

The nursing home allowed smoking only in designated areas. Pop obliged by smoking only where allowed. He retained a semblance of respect for non-smokers rights. Mom seemed oblivious that smoking might be detrimental to others and herself. She continued to drop ashes and burn holes in her clothes. She refused to smoke only where allowed and lit up wherever she chose.

The nursing home staff and I had a consultation. It was decided to restrict her smoking to those times when she could be adequately supervised. I quickly recognized this was a declaration of war.

"Mom, I think we have a problem with your smoking," I told her. "Look at the holes in your clothes. They're from cigarettes." I thought it best to approach the situation by pandering to her instincts for self-preservation. Surely she didn't want to burn her clothes or hurt herself, I thought.

"That's a bunch of crap," was her immediate response. "I've always smoked and nothing bad has happened." She lit up another cigarette.

I tried a different approach.

"Most of the people living here don't smoke and cigarette smoke really bothers them," I told her.

I hoped that she might condescend and show consideration for other people.

"To hell with them," was her reply.

She insisted on smoking. She interpreted any restrictions or others people's objections as a challenge. Her constitutional rights were being violated. She would fight back. She would prevail. She refused to move from the smoking room and continued chain smoking.

"If they don't like it, they can go to hell," she responded. She repudiated being told what to do.

Staff members took away her cigarettes. They confiscated her lighters. They allowed her to smoke only when supervised. She begged for cigarettes from other residents. She continued to explode with hissy fits, but to no avail. She seethed and sulked. She accused my father of colluding with the enemy when he refused to give her cigarettes. She bribed other smokers. She became abusive to some residents, pulling the hair of one lady, and socking another on the back of the head. One time she managed to take all the staff time cards from their slots and rip them to pieces. The time clock had to be moved to a different location. Smoking was her crusade and she refused to acquiesce.

It was a battle of wills. I felt compassion for Mom knowing how hard it must be to kick an addiction. Persistence and the necessity for safety eventually won out. Mom didn't stop smoking but did cease her uncooperative and destructive behavior. She accepted begrudgingly the limitations set upon her smoking. For both Mom and Pop, smoking continued as their primary preoccupation.

* * * *

I have always considered adultery unethical, to say the least. For a married person to form a loving relationship with another person and act on that relationship must be the antithesis of moral responsibility. But even the best ethical judgments can be subject to scrutiny – it depends on the situation.

Romancing Rita

"I need to talk with you Peter," were the first words from Pop the day I arrived for a regular visit. He met me at the front door. He appeared anxious and fidgety. He kept wiping his brow despite that it was not a warm day. "We need to talk privately," he continued.

Private conversations with Pop were preludes to resolving problems. They were set ups for failure. It proved extremely difficult to resolve a problem for him to his satisfaction. Any suggested resolution was quickly rejected Most of his problems centered on Mom. She was driving him crazy. She followed him around the nursing home like a puppy dog. She constantly asked for cigarettes. Despite knowing that she was quickly losing many of her metal faculties, he was torn between caring about her and the annoyances of someone with creeping dementia.

"Peter, I need to talk with you privately," he persisted. I consented reluctantly and we walked down the hall toward his room. He was still living separately from Mom, in the same building but in a different wing. He had his own room as part of a new section for residents who needed only some assistance. Mom was a full care nursing home resident.

We entered his room and sat on the bed. After a slight pause when neither of us spoke, Pop said, "She has never been right in her mind and now its worse."

"You mean Mom?" I asked.

"Yes, your mother." He exclaimed with the usual litany of old memories justifying his explanation.

"When I gave her a wedding ring sixty years ago, she got mad and threw it at me saying it was too cheap. She gets angry and blames me for everything. I've taken good care of her, supported her all these years and she still is not satisfied that I pay her enough attention. Do you think I neglect her?' he asked me.

"No," I replied.

"I try to be kind to her, but it's so hard now that she acts so crazy like."

"It's the dementia. It's like a sickness with her. She can't help that," I reminded him.

"I know, I know," he told me. "But sometimes I just can't stand to be with her."

There was another period of silence.

"It's not easy to be alone, you know," Pop said.

Since I had heard much of this speech during the last few months, I considered it a prelude to something else he wanted to tell me.

"I have a girl friend, "Pop blurted out. "I suppose you are going to be mad at me, but I found a girl friend."

"Who's that? I asked.

"Rita," he said. He then began a lengthy description of the history of himself and Rita. He had known her many years. She was the wife of a roommate from his high school years with whom both he and Mom had kept in touch. They met at reunions and occasionally socialized together when they lived close by.

Rita's husband had died recently. Pop learned about this from reading his high school alumni magazine. He called her. Then he called her again.

"Now I talk with her almost every evening," he told me. "She is very nice."

He wanted to "experience a relationship with her" is how he described it.

"She is warm and accepting. She doesn't want anything from me. We just share confidences." He used words I never imagined would come from him.

Their conversations were about feelings, about what they did that day or were planning to do the next day. "We share how we are feeling about stuff, about ourselves." It was mostly small talk, but he told me it made him feel good.

"I think I am in love with her," he confessed. He sounded sincere, but I sensed a twinge of guilt in his voice.

And then he added, "How do you feel about this? Are you mad at me because you think I'm cheating on your mother?"

Because I didn't answer right away, Pop continued. "Rita is sweet. I don't have to explain myself to her. I like to talk with her and I don't have to take care of her."

All this from a phone conversation, I wondered.

I wasn't sure how to respond. It took me by surprise. The last thing I ever would have imagined was to hear Pop talk intimately about another woman. I didn't remember him ever doing so with Mom.

I knew he had grown weary of care taking Mom, even with the help of the nursing home staff. He had a strong sense of responsibility toward her and I didn't imagine him abandoning her despite the annoyance he felt. His feelings toward Mom were now born out of a conflict between guilt and commitment. That was implicit in his confession.

"It's fine with me," I told him. It really wasn't fine but I felt I had to say something to assuage his guilt and not upset him. When they moved into the assisted living facility, I had hoped that age and circumstance might mellow them a bit, that growing old together would soften their hostility and intolerance, and they would discover a new sense of companionship. They remained companions mostly out of necessity, but I sensed little affection.

"Don't worry about it," I added as a way of transitioning from this subject to another. I could muster no rational arguments nor pronounce any judgments at the moment. I wanted to leave the topic and make time later to digest it.

"If this makes you feel happy and content then go ahead and talk with her." I told him before deciding to excuse myself by telling him I had to go and we would talk again later. I was thinking that this might pass; I hoped that it was just a phase and in a few days or weeks it would all be history. Any harm done would be minimal.

When Pop said he wanted to call Rita regularly, I had no idea how often this would be. When I got his next phone bill, I saw that most days he called her twice. True to his spirit, the phone calls became a part of Pop's routine. Each day would be scheduled in such a way to make specific times available to call Rita right after lunch and diner.

I said nothing to Mom about Pop's romancing of Rita. I doubted she would understand or remember. I continued to feel conflicted about the relationship as if somehow I was complicit in the affair. Pop still sat with Mom briefly after each meal but returned to his room in haste to call Rita as scheduled. I felt uncomfortable when sitting with both of them together knowing that Pop had a girl friend. This feeling wasn't to last long, however. After a few months of not discussing the circumstances, I happen to ask Pop when we were alone, "How's it going with Rita?"

"Don't call her much anymore," he said. I didn't ask why. I didn't respond at all. I let it go completely. Nothing was ever mentioned about Rita again.

In a recent article in the AARP Magazine (November 2011, pp.81-82), it was stated that because of recent developments in the lives or caretakers, many professionals, even some religious leaders, have redefined adultery. Dementia, in its many and varied forms, can persist through a long life-time, some say up to twenty years. That's a long time for either partner in a marriage to survive without the intimacy of the one with the disease. More and more care takers are choosing to look for and find significant others to fulfill the need for closeness and affection that is missing in the relationship. Yes, it might be stretching the vow of "to love and cherish through health and in sickness" but it might also prove necessary for the mental health of the caretaker.

The ethics of these new relationships are being touted by some in the religious arena. The televangelist Pat Robertson remarked, "I can't fault (the man) for wanting some kind of companionship. This is the person you have loved for 20, 30, 40 years and suddenly that person is gone." (Quoted in AARP Magazine, November 2011, p.82)

Many, if not most, of those suffering the ravages of dementia or Alzheimer's have lost recognition of the marriage partner. Some, as a result of their memory loss, even attempt to start new relationships with people they hardly know who might be sharing the same care facility. The point being, it must prove terribly hard to hold together a relationship devoid of all forms of intimacy and recognition and at the same time hold together your own sense of wholeness as a person.

Perhaps the key element in whether adultery is an issue depends upon the attitude of the caretaker. If the new relationship is a "diversion" rather than "abandonment", adultery may not become a moral and ethical issue. Some say that as long as the caretaker in the relationships does not abandon responsibility for providing loving care of the other, then the new relationship fulfills a need that the marriage partner can not oblige. A relationship outside the bonds of marriage is still an issue, but an understandable one under the circumstances.

I don't propose that any conditions be altered in the marriage relationship or the commitments made "for a life time", rather that consideration is given to the circumstances and that the ethics is understood as "situational." Blanket condemnation is neither healthy nor fair. For Pop, his new girl friend was a temporary experience, soon forgotten. For many others whose soul mate is suffering from Alzheimer's or other forms of dementia, the possibility of a dual commitment looms always in the background.

Mom's Red Dress

There was only a single closet in each room at the nursing home. Mom shared a room with another lady. Regardless of how much clothing each had, only half the closet was available for storage.

Before Mom entered the home, I suggested that she sort her clothing. I asked that she give me anything she didn't want anymore and I would donate it "in her name" to the local Salvation Army.

"I need it all," she told me.

"But there is not much room in the closet for all your clothes. You have to share the space with your roommate," I responded.

"To hell with her," Mom said. "I need my own closet."

That was my first hint that Mom was not going to be a cooperative roommate, willing to share much of anything with someone else living in her space. Despite her objections, I was able to eliminate a large portion of her clothes. The remainder I had to mark with her name with an indelible pen before stowing in the closet.

"I'm used to having my own closet," she added. "What if she takes some of my things? That's horrible, I don't like it."

This confirmed my hunch that having a roommate would not be an easy adjustment. I tried to reassure her that it would all work nicely, that she would enjoy the company, and I was positive that her room mate was a good, honest person. Of course, that was an embellishment as I had no idea of her roommate's history. For as much as I knew she could have been recently released from a psychiatric hospital. I had not yet met her and was only told by the staff that she was a "nice" lady. The staff referred to all the old people as "nice."

It must be difficult, I thought, to have spent so many years in your own room in your own house with all the closet space you wanted for your personal things and then to be subjected overnight to a single room with only half a closet and a new roommate. To lose that sense of personal dignity, I suspect, is among the hardest transitions a person must make.

Recognizing spiritual distress is often most difficult. It is particularly so for a person suffering the throes of dementia. Under normal circumstances, the person might address the problem directly. "I am feeling very uncomfortable and fearful of these changes in my life" or "This is not what I am used to and it causes me great stress." For the person with dementia, simple and direct communication is more than a challenge, it is almost impossible. We can get hints of their spiritual distress less by their words and more by their actions. The disturbance in Mom's life became evidenced by her displeasure at having to share space with another person, a stranger, an experience far removed from her usual comfort zone. Mom quickly recognized this as upsetting but was not able to articulate her displeasure. Her actions of rebellion and repulsiveness clearly hint at spiritual distress much more so than any words she might be able to muster.

I carefully placed Mom's limited assortment of dresses, sweaters, slacks, and tops in her side of the closet. It took ingenuity to get them all in properly so they didn't interfere with her roommate's space. The closet was packed full, making it difficult to withdraw one dress without upsetting all the others.

"I don't like these old dresses anyway, so you might as well give them away," she told me as I was about to leave. Her change of mind surprised me. She seemed unaware that I had already decimated her stock of dresses. The ones in the closet were the only one's remaining. I suspect she didn't mean what she was saying. It was her way of resigning herself to her new situation with a lingering disapproval. She acquiesced.

As she grew older, Mom could only manage dresses that easily slipped over her head. Buttons required too much agility and were beyond her ability. Getting her into underwear proved to be a considerable chore. Shoes and socks were even more difficult. She didn't like the indignity of having staff help her. Her solution was to dress simply. Slip on dresses, no zippers, no buttons, and no fasteners of any sort. Only two colors suited her, red and blue. She insisted that underwear be white, but everything else red or blue. She particularly liked red.

Shopping for dresses with Mom fell into a routine. She often suggested we go shopping, but only occasionally would I agree.

"I need a new dress. The stuff I have is all falling apart. When can we go shopping?" she would ask continually.

"Soon," I would reply. "Soon as I can get some time."

When I could no longer delay her insistence, I settled on an afternoon for dress shopping.

"Do you want to look at blue dresses," I asked her as we entered Weiners, the mature women's dress shop. It was our favorite because of the huge selection suited for the "mature" woman.

"Only if they don't have a red one I like," Mom answered.

We only looked at red dresses. I knew the consequences if I convinced her to buy a blue dress. The next day she would insist that we return the blue dress and look again for a red one.

Mom did not know her size. I could only guess. Women's clothing sizes were enigmas to me. They appeared to bear no resemblance to any mathematics I understood.

"I wear medium," she replied when I asked her size. "I always take a medium." She insisted she *always* wore medium despite being considerable larger at this stage of her life. Not all women's dresses are marked "medium." Some have particular sizes marked on them – 12, 14, and 18. I had to figure out how to transpose a particular size that corresponded to medium.

Mom's circumstance posed a particular problem. She preferred to use a wheelchair. Standing up was difficult.

When she did stand, she was unsteady. Trying on dresses the usual way – taking them into a fitting room – was not possible. It was by holding the dress in front of her that I estimated, better yet guessed, that it would fit. If I missed the mark, we had to do the shopping all over again.

"I like this one," Mom exclaimed upon finding a red dress. So long as it was red, it mattered little what other attributes it had. Size was not her concern.

"But Mom, this is a petite," I explained while trying not to hurt her feelings. I reminded her that petite was for high school girls. She accepted my rational and we moved on to other categories.

Eventually we found three or four dresses in various shades of red and approximately her size with no buttons and no zippers and no tight waist lines. While Mom remained in her wheelchair, I attempted to wiggle the dresses over her head to be sure that at least the top part fit her properly. Her bottom part was about the same size as her top, at least in girth, so I figured if it fit over her shoulders it would fit over middle. I held up several for her inspection.

She liked the dresses.

"I want to buy them all," she told me. It sounded like a demand but was said more with a sense of anticipation expecting my approval.

"Why don't we take just two for now," I explained. "We don't have enough money for all of them."

"But the red ones won't be here later if we don't take them now," she said. Mom became insistent. Despite her dementia, I was amazed at her comprehension.

It was time to negotiate. "How about we buy two today and that will give us a reason to go shopping again another day. I am sure they will have more red dresses later," was my suggestion.

Mom was a bit suspicious. "When will we go again?" she asked.

"Just as soon as I can get some time away from work," I answered. Work was my excuse for not being able to do what she wanted exactly when she wanted to do it. I was reluctant to buy four dresses at one time, but found reasoning with

Mom to be impossible. Empty promises to come again "real soon" seemed to placate her best.

Mom bought the compromise. I bought the two dresses. I suspect that Mom was well aware that she was not going to get four dresses but figured that if she asked for them all, a compromise would be reached at two. Sometimes Mom pretended to be unaware, but actually knew precisely what she was doing. Dementia is not always plagued by ignorance.

Those more familiar with the role of spirituality in life than me comment that for the aging population there is an emphasis on internal processes which facilitate expanding consciousness. In brief, this may mean that the elderly devote more time to meditate, fantasize, and participate in more passive activities. As they contemplate and reflect, it can stimulate a healthier life style, both physically and emotionally. Sometimes Mom and Pop took this advice to the extremes. They developed fascinations where fascinations need not necessarily be focused.

Bowels

Bowels are the barometer of life. Their regularity is essential to health and happiness. When I was younger, I never gave much thought to intestines, mine or other people's. What happened after I ate was of little concern outside of how well it tasted and whether I felt full. I occasionally suffered from mild bouts of constipation or diarrhea. Sometimes gas became a problem, mostly to the other people nearby. Beyond these consideration, my lower G.I. tract generated less interest than, say, tooth decay or corns on my feet.

From the gospel according to Mom and Pop, I learned bowels held the key to health and happiness. The proper functioning of the colon, the urinary tract, and lower digestive pathway was nature's omen of telling us that all is well in the universe. I heard about every conceivable problem that one might encounter with the bowels. They both became enslaved to the activity or inactivity of their G.I tracts.

Mom was obsessed with her colon, especially while she still lived in the apartment. She worried incessantly about its proper functioning. Hardly a week passed without her experiencing discomforting levels of intestinal cramps, constipation, or diarrhea. She insisted on calling a doctor. When she told him she was severely constipated, the doctor would prescribe a laxative with instruction to follow the label on the bottle. Ignoring the doctor's orders, Mom swallowed nearly the whole bottle at once.

Another call to the doctor. This time she complained of diarrhea. She messed her underwear and couldn't control her bowels. She needed relief immediately. The doctor prescribed a bottle of Peptin and instructed her to follow the bottle instructions. Mom decided if a little medicine helped a little, a lot of medicine would help a lot. She consumed almost the entire bottle. It cured the diarrhea, but constipation soon reoccurred. The pattern of constipation followed by diarrhea followed by constipation ad nausea continued.

With the help of a nutrition staff at the nursing home, the pattern was broken. A diet of whole grains, vegetables, and dairy products eventually gave Mom the relief she graved.

My father's fascination with bowels took a different twist. He became obsessed with urination. Pop maintained that people were programmed to urinate at specific times each day. Feeling the urge was an indication, but not as important a factor as maintaining a routine.

Pop's biological rhythms demanded that he pee the first thing each morning, again at eleven o'clock, right after lunch, once again in the late afternoon, and always just before bedtime. There was to be no alternative scheduling. Much to his chagrin, as he grew older, his urges failed to meet his schedule. It became downright catastrophic when urination was irregular.

I visited Pop many times in the early evening. He retired before eight o'clock most nights. He was in bed, pajamas on, television on, and Tylenol sleeping pills and a glass of water at his bedside. I looked directly at him and noticed immediately a cringe of agony on his face. His eyes were squinted, his face contorted, and he had a look of forlorn on his face.

"What's the matter, Pop?" I asked.

"It's this urination crap," he said. "I got to take a piss and I can't. It's time but I can't piss."

I watched as he reached down with both hands and massaged his abdomen, pushing down slightly while grimacing in pain.

"What are you doing that for, Pop?" I asked him

"I'm trying to push the piss out," he told me.

"Do you really have to go badly?" I asked

"Not right at the moment," he responded. "But it's time. Otherwise I can't get to sleep."

I tried convincing Mom and Pop that the more they worried about their bowels; the less likely they would function properly. I was never sure of my diagnosis or remedy, but their anxiety seemed unwarranted and only caused more aggravation. I learned that if you truly want to be a good care giver of aging parents, never underestimate the power and potency of bowels.

A person's spirituality is linked to their sense of identity. Even more than consideration of one's talents and abilities, ones awareness of being accepted and loved is important content of one's spiritual assessment. To be without anyone who's proven love and care is present is to be without a healthy spirituality. A person's spirituality can be found at the root of every conversation, action, and expressed emotion.

Spiritual distress may also be easily recognized. Such distress is evidence by a disturbance in the value system that provides the person with strength of character and confidence in personal identity. Such distress is noticeable by a constant yearning to know that one is appreciated, loved, and recognized as important by those around him. I observed this trait in my father on many occasions.

Pop often demanded more of my attention than Mom. On those occasions when I intended to visit with both of them, I ended up in extended conversations with my father. Since Mom was slowly drifting into dementia, her ability to communicate was becoming more limited. She did not demand much from a conversation. Having another cigarette was her priority. Pop, however, used the time to vent his frustrations.

While conversations with Mom were limited both in time and place – only at the nursing home – Pop made contact with me at home as well as at the nursing facility. He often attempted to isolate me from Mom so that he could reveal some problem or concern that had been festering with him for some time. I became quite impressed by his ability to manipulate, which I didn't consider was done intentionally to annoy, but rather as an exercise in testing my commitment and love.

My primary preoccupation with my father was to seek out any and all opportunities to provide him with personal well being, contentment, and serenity. He was not a happy camper and never an easy person to please. It wasn't that he required much attention. Rather it was that he had a low tolerance level. Too much noise, a broken routine, annoyances from Mom, interruptions from other residents; there was no end to what irritated him and disrupted his day.

He was not one to keep these annoyances to himself. His venting, however, was usually in my direction. The feeling I got from him was that I was responsible for solving his dilemmas. Included in almost every conversation was his mandate, "Peter, you need to do something about this." The frustration I felt was most often less about fixing the problem and more often that no solution would provide him with the peace and contentment for which he wish so desperately.

The Importance of Routine

There is a direct connection between spirituality and routine. I didn't always believe this, but after considerable observation of what seems to make life bearable for my aging father, I now know of its worth. Routine allows one to live in the middle where it's safe, away from the threat of the unexpected, far from the harsh edges where one might abruptly fall off into an abyss. Life is at its most dangerous when it's lived near the edges – that's where the tragedies happen. For the older person, constantly threatened with the termination of life, sickness and emotional downs, spiritual and emotional security occurs only where there is safety.

Once a routine is established, life becomes safe and comfortable. Routines give people security. Routines reduce anxiety and fear of the future. With a routine, a person remains in control. Life becomes predictable. One knows what to expect.

Spirituality can be deepened by repetition and routine. Routine is calming and introspective when repetitive acts are done as part of one's religion – repeating a simple mantra or fingering beads during prayer. Someone once asked the Dalai Lama if there where one thing he could recommend for living the fulfilling life. He responded "routines." Many "experts" with knowledge about living a long and prosperous life site practicing routine as a major contributing factor.

My father practiced the art of the routine like a real champion. I will never know if he associated it with spirituality, but I do know that his routine held special significance for him. Pop was a slave to the routine. The older he became the more entrenched became his addiction to his routine. His life focused on maintaining his daily regimens. Regular life patterns gave structure to his life and control over his environment. Spiritual routines, however, can easily become ruts when they remain so unchanging that one engages in them mindlessly. Pop often fell into that trap.

Pop thrived on controlling his routines but his slavish addiction also allowed his routines to control him. Whenever these daily patterns were altered in the slightest manner, he acted confused and bewildered, anxious and angry. While living at the nursing home, Pop established routines for every aspect of his life – eating, sleeping, entertainment, place, and bathroom etiquette. Any disruption caused disorientation, nausea, severe anxiety, constipation, agitation, jitteriness, and all around general uneasiness.

Meals provided the foundation for daily routine. At the nursing home breakfast was at 7:00 A.M., lunch at noon, and supper, not dinner, at 5:30 P.M. This was required. When it varied his demeanor became highly distressed. When both Mom and Pop were still ambulatory I would have them over to my house for a lunch or supper. It was often difficult, especially when our kids were present, to arrange for meals times as Pop expected. Immediately his agitation was aroused. His resistance was of the passive/aggressive type. He would walk into the kitchen and stand there staring at the stove as if to hurry the cooking process.

"How's supper coming?" he would ask. "Almost ready?"

Pop grumbled under his breath, but just loud enough for me to hear his dissatisfaction. "I'm gonna miss the news on television."

"We're almost there Pop," I would respond, knowing that his level of agitation and anxiety would certainly increase with each passing moment.

The predictability of meals times at the nursing home suited Pop well. I asked why he felt it so important that he eat at such structured times.

"That's when they serve the food," he would answer. "Besides if I have things to do after lunch or after supper I can't do them until I have lunch or supper." That made sense to me. He planned the rest of his day in accordance with meal times – a nap following lunch, reading in the parlor the hour before supper, the television news immediately after supper. I thought his insistence about regular meal times might lesson the longer he lived in the nursing home but it only increased. He became more adamant.

When they lived in the apartment, in an effort to provide some variety in his life, I often took him and Mom for rides in the country on Sunday afternoons. I considered it might be a welcomed diversion from the monotony of home life. I paid scant attention to time. As the afternoon progressed I sensed a building agitation from Pop.

"How do you like these wild flowers?" I asked.

"They are nice, but don't you think it best if we start back?" Pop would reply.

I looked at my watch. It was approaching 4:30 P.M. I immediately understood that he was anxious that we might not return in time for his supper. It wasn't that he needed supper to satisfy his hunger, but supper was a time marker in his routine for Sundays. Supper at 5:30 so he would be ready for the *60 Minutes* television show which he watched religiously. It had to be in that order. No amount of appeasement would alter this routine. Nothing existed that could persuade him otherwise.

The routine of place held an equally significant spiritual value although not acknowledged by Pop. Where he spent his time at the nursing home contributed to his feeling of well being as much his routine of time allotments. Certain events happen at certain times and in certain places. Pop had particular places he needed to be in order to bring comfort and security to his life.

He claimed "his chair" in the front room of the home. There were many sofas and chairs in the room, but only one suited him. It was next to the window. It was there he had to sit each morning following breakfast to read his newspaper. He occupied the same chair at the same time in the same place or all was not right with the world. Many times I was told by staff that if another person happened to occupy that particular chair at that time, Pop would not hesitate to remind the occupant of his errant ways and he expected him to move to another chair.

Substitutions for reading materials were not allowed. His routine for reading was chronologically specific. After breakfast, he preferred the newspaper. Following lunch he read either the National Geographic, the Readers Digest, Life magazine, or Yankee Magazine. He read them usually in that order. No substitutes here either. The nursing home had accumulated a plethora of back issues, enough to last his expected life time. After supper, he didn't read. He claimed it was too hard to see without day light. Instead that was his television news hour.

There was only one television in the front living room of the nursing home. While Pop had little interest in watching during daylight, when evening came he became quite possessive of his news hour. He had no hesitation, much to the chagrin of other residents, of intentionally changing the channel despite that others might have already decided on a specific show. No one argued with him. Eventually, I bought him a small television he could place in his room. This only added to his absence from Mom.

Pop didn't read books. "The library here and downtown has lots of good travel books," I often reminded him. "You can read about places you know or have been to."

"Books are too long," he responded. "I am never sure I will live long enough to finish a book."

Routine ruled Pop's life. Nothing was as important as adhering to a regimen.

If he needed a doctor's appointment, he pestered me until I scheduled it between meal times or before or after nap time or late morning after the newspaper hour. Once we arrived at the doctor's office and the nurse informed us that the doctor was running late, Pop insisted we leave and reschedule. Waiting would have encroached on his routine. He only agreed to have eye surgery if an appointment could be scheduled between meal times and if I could guarantee that he would be home at the proper time. Fortunately, this proved possible and eye surgery was completed.

It took some adjustment on my part, but I learned to respect Pop's routines. I understood it was not simply a slavish adherence to a monotonous groove that he had fallen into accidentally. It was intentional, a way of ordering experiences, providing focus, and guaranteeing security.

As a spiritual aspect of our lives routines serve specific purposes. We develop daily patterns that best meet the circumstances that reflect present conditions- our work schedules, our children's growing experiences, our needs for recreation and leisure activities, the seasons of the year. We formalize routines only for the present time and to meet present circumstances. Otherwise they become the nemesis of our existence. Despite occasionally seeking activities that are radically diverse, we quickly resume our routines before feelings of anxiety and vulnerably overwhelm us.

For older people, like my father, specific patterns of daily living are like a pair of old shoes. They are comfortable. I can understand the adamant refusal of all attempts to rid themselves of routines unless absolutely necessary, and then only begrudgingly. It may not be a conscious effort, but rather a subconscious attempt to maintain what little dignity and self control they can preserve. Comfort brings contentment and contentment is a primary ingredient of the spiritual life.

No More Testicles

I thought Pop would go through the roof when he heard his testicles had to be removed. I was dead wrong. He had no objections. The news didn't faze him in the slightest. I might have told him he needed a tooth filled or his toenails needed cutting.

His attitude was positive. Perhaps he sensed that removing his testicles would provide him some relief from sore legs and his urination problem. He had been "reamed out" as he called it, twice before so that he could pee more easily. That's when I knew he didn't realize what I was talking about.

Pop had difficulty urinating. He claimed it was too hard to pee when he thought he ought to be peeing. He described his condition as being blocked up. If he could get "reamed out"– having the inside of his penis cleaned – he would be fine. It was Pop's terminology for a procedure he didn't fully understand but knew the desired consequences. Pops understanding of human plumbing left much to be desired.

I explained the procedure to him as best I was able with my limited knowledge. He needed to know the truth, to know exactly what was to happen. It was a matter of integrity, his right to know. I still hesitated to be specific for fear of discouraging or frightening him. He had positive expectations; I didn't want to discourage his hopefulness.

"Pop, the doctor says that your leg pains are probably caused by the advancing prostate cancer," I told him. "He thinks that…" Suddenly I was interrupted.

"What cancer? I don't have cancer. What are you talking about?" Pop said. "My problem is I can't piss when I want to. I just need to get reamed out. That's always worked before and I'm good for a long time. That's all I need. There ain't nothing to this cancer stuff." Pop was adamant.

I tried reasoning.

"This is not just a reaming out operation," I almost yelled. I wanted to get through to him. "You do have prostrate cancer. Don't you remember? You've had it for many years. Removing your testicles will arrest the spread of cancer and hopefully alleviate some of the pain in your legs you keep complaining about." I wanted to be empathetic but also wanted him to fully understand. "And that's not all," I added. "They want you to have radiation therapy after the operation."

I might as well have told him he had to jump from the Brooklyn Bridge. He didn't take this news well.

"Wait a minute. Just one minute here. What's this radiation stuff? I'm not taking any radiation, not unless it's over my dead body."

I had Pop's attention.

"After they remove your testicles, you'll need to have radiation on your prostate. They have to do this to be sure the cancer is all gone there. It kinda burns up the entire residue." I wasn't sure I was being accurate, but I was on a roll.

"What do you mean? Make sure all what is gone?" he asked me.

"We will have to go to the hospital once each week for treatments. I think it will take a couple of months." I told him.

"How much time will it take? He asked.

"I don't know for sure," I said. "We will have to go to San Antonio once each week and with travel time and waiting and other stuff, it might be most of the day."

From his questions, I thought he was warming to the idea.

"Naw, I'm not going to do that. I don't need radiation. They just need to ream me out," he insisted. I got the distinct feeling Pop was unyielding and there was no use in pleading with him.

Pop agreed to have his testicles removed, but nothing else. This, he reasoned, was no more serious than having a wart removed. He claimed he didn't need them anymore, so good riddance. After a day and a half, he was released to go home.

It took a while, but eventually I realized Pop's rational for refusing radiation treatment. He was beyond fearing its consequence. The actual treatments didn't faze him. It was the time involved; time that would upset his routine. Upsetting Pop's routine was paramount to treason. He would never agree to missing his morning newspaper or not having his dinner at 5:30 or his afternoon nap at 1:00. Radiation therapy meant long drives to the city, extended waiting time, possible nausea preventing his eating, and daily time changes all of which would cause disruption in his routine. That was not to be. No therapy.

"Besides," Pop added. "Those doctors are a bunch of butchers. They don't know what they are doing. They just like doing operations so they can make more money."

Pop's pain-free, sickness-free, and accident-free life had conditioned him to be un-accepting of medical treatments, especially when they threatened to upset his routine. Until the past few years, the most medication he had ever taken was a few aspirin and mouthwash. He was convinced that over the counter medications, "the kind from Rexalls" was sufficient. His suspicion of prescription drugs never waned despite that he took some now. He did so only reluctantly.

"Peter," he told me on numerous occasions after the operation to remove his testicles, "I have only a few years left. I don't plan to have a bunch of doctors screw up my routine of things I like to do." And that was that.

What Pop thought of when he heard the word healing was cure; he wanted to be cured of what ailed him. He wanted life to return to the way it had always been. Sometimes being fully cured is not possible, but healing still remains an option. Healing can also come through coping. For my father, coping carried the meaning of "giving in" an attitude he was adamantly opposed to. The resulting circumstances meant that if he could not do something the way he was used to doing it, it had to be abandoned altogether.

No amount of rational could convince Pop that coping was a strategy that might allow him to integrate a new way of life to substitute for the old way. If he enjoyed gardening while he was able to walk the grounds, lift heavy equipment, and bend over unceasingly, he didn't have to abandon his love of gardening; he merely had to find another way of accomplishing the same task, perhaps in a limited way, but still in a manner that he could enjoy. Pop rejected outright this perspective. If he could look inward to his source of spirituality, he would have discovered that life does not end when one activity is curtailed. Spiritual resources can make sense of life when the physical breaks down.

＊ ＊ ＊ ＊

Pop was not good at coping. Pop's perspective on change was that it ought not to happen, especially to him. Change was his enemy. Change meant learning to cope, finding another way to accomplish the same thing, having to do it differently than you used to do it. Whenever Pop confronted change, particularly physical change, he wanted to experience healing, to be cured, to be restored to the way things used to be. The idea of coping, managing new experiences in new ways, held no appeal to Pop.

Healthy spirituality includes the possibility of coping. It is to allow the new situation in which I find myself to become integrated into a new way of life. Life does not end when one can no longer walk. Our spirituality reminds us that there is still something new breaking into life, even as old parts wither away. By all accounts, Pop was not able to comprehend this or to incorporate this thinking into his attitudes and beliefs. If he could not do something the way he had always done it, then he would not do it at all. This attitude carried over to other aspects of his life.

The scooter fiasco

"I just can't do this anymore," Pop announced at the beginning of my regular visit time. It was Wednesday afternoon.

"Can't do what? I asked

"Can't walk," he responded. "My legs hurt too much."

Six months ago he moved back into the assisted living apartment adjacent to the nursing home. He had been staying at the nursing home on a wing reserved specifically for ambulatory residents who needed minimal care – bed making, medication management, laundry service, etc. He decided he could manage on his own. I suspect the real reason was for respite care from Mom. Mom lived in her own room at the home but had discovered where Pop's room was and constantly pestered him for cigarettes. He decided to make the move. At the apartment, he could nap when he wanted, watch television uninterrupted, and read in quiet apart from Mom. He still returned to the home for his noon and evening meals.

"Peter, what am I going to do? Walking back and forth just makes my legs ache," he told me. His faced grimaced to emphasize his agony. He pulled back his lips to show clenched teeth, his usual sign of agitation and pain. I think the thought of his dilemma further perturbed him. Most times his anxiety caused him more emotional agitation than physical pain. His expression and tone needed immediate translation. Was he hurting physically or just angry and upset?

We were sitting in the front room of the nursing home. He was about to go back to his apartment, but decided upon a cigarette break before proceeding. Mom was already in her own room. A long ash from the cigarette was about to drop on to the floor. I moved an ash tray toward him. He snuffed the cigarette out.

"I like where I am living, what with your mother being like she is, " he continued, "but it's getting too hard to walk back and forth. So what am I supposed to do?"

He looked directly at me and paused as if expecting an answer to be forthcoming immediately.

I gave no answer. I had no answer to give.

Since moving into the apartment, I detected a new sense of independence from Pop. His reliance upon me as a "fixer" for what was wrong with his life greatly diminished. I was thankful. Nor did he shirk his responsibility as a husband. He intentionally spent time with Mom at meals and a brief sojourn following before he retreated. He hardly talked to her except to reprimand her for bumping her wheelchair into his legs and constantly asking for a cigarette. I suspected his presence with her relieved him of guilt. Overall his contentment factor rose.

Today he was persistent. "Peter, you've got to help me," he repeated. The question was addressed directly to me. He wasn't wondering aloud. He expected an answer.

Pop was diagnosed with prostate cancer nearly a decade previously. He claims he forgot or that I was mistaken whenever I reminded him. Denial was his way of dealing with the inevitable when it was bad news. The prognosis was that he would eventually experience pain in his legs. I mentioned this again to him, but his reaction was stoic.

As long as the cancer didn't upset his routine, he paid it no attention.

"It's not cancer," he responded. It's just pain in my legs because I'm too old."

I knew it was more serious than he anticipated or would admit. I imagined the worst. Was he going to die soon? My "awfulizing" went into high gear? It would be a painful death, painful for him and painful for me watching him. I found it difficult to not think first about my responsibility. What demands would be made of me? Selfish perhaps, but true.

I remember asking the doctor back when he was first diagnosed.

"How serious is his condition?"

"Oh, it's serious," the doctor replied. "It could cause him considerable pain down the road. However, it's more likely he'll die from being hit by a Mack truck in the next ten years than from this cancer. It's very slow growing. Don't need to do a lot of worrying." I read some literature about prostate cancer that informed me that leg pain is a common symptom. This was his diagnosis nearly a decade ago. I figured now the cancer was beginning to catch up to him despite that his testicles were removed.

"Peter, what am I going to do now?" Pop repeated again.

"Let's get one of those motorized scooters." The idea struck me spontaneously. I thought it brilliant. "You can use it to get back and forth from the apartment. It will save you from walking and you'll still be mobile." I waited for a response.

"That sounds pretty stupid, I don't think so," he told me. There was a bit of irony in his voice as if he had thought of the idea previously and dismissed it.

"Why not?" I said. "It's a solution to your problem. You asked me what you should do. Here's a suggestion and you don't like it." His flat rejection caught me by surprise. I felt ignored.

There was silence for a moment and then he showed a brief acknowledgment of acceptance. "Where do you suppose you will get one of those?"

It didn't take long. I located the perfect solution. It was a three-wheeled motorized chair with bicycle type hand controls. The forward, backward, and speed control was a single lever. It could maneuver around corners easily and had the power to climb up slight inclines. Its top speed was slightly faster than a brisk walk. The swivel seat had a removable arm rest allowing effortless entry and exit. It was a shinny fire engine red. It didn't come with a crash helmet.

"He'll love it," I thought. I bought it.

He didn't love it.

"I can't use that damn thing," was his immediate response when I brought it to the home.

"It's easy," I reassured him. "Any damn fool can use it." There was a hint of anger in my voice in reaction to his immediate rejection. "Let me show you." I got on the scooter, drove it around the sitting room, down the hall, turned around, came back to where he was sitting, and parked it at his feet. "Now you do it," I said. I was determined, not willing to take no for an answer.

"I can't learn to use that. It's too complicated. I'm too old to learn now," Pop responded just as insistently.

"I just showed you how easy it is." I repeated. "Just give it a try, that's all I'm asking. Do a few practice runs while I'm here to help. If you don't like it, I can return it." Pop never asked where I bought the scooter or how much it cost.

"You sure you can return it?" he asked.

"Of course, but you have to give it a try first. That's part of the deal. If it doesn't work for you I promise I'll get rid of it." That was a shallow promise. I had no intention of returning the scooter as I felt very confident he would eventually adjust to using it. One or two trips back and forth from the apartment and he would be hooked and delighted. I reminded him that the whole facility was barrier free. He could come and go without restrictions – back to his room for naps, to the dining room for meals, out side for a smoke. I added "you can get away from Mom easier with this." I thought to myself, *"If walking is your agony, then damn it, this scooter is your salvation."*

Pop still looked hesitant.

"Come on Pop. I spent a lot of time and energy getting this thing up here." I pleaded with him. "The least you can do is try it out for a while." I hoped to work on his guilt. "Let's give it a try, Okay?"

He didn't respond. I took that as a yes.

I surveyed a section of the nursing home that was open and accessible. A few items of furniture were scattered about the room, near enough to be challenges but far enough apart not to be hindrances. He could test his skill. Pop slid into the seat. He griped the handlebars and gingerly depressed the forward handle. Nothing happened.

"Squeeze it firmly," I advised him.

He squeezed it harder and suddenly, like a rocket, the chair lurched forward at great speed.

"Peter," he yelled. "This is too fast." He had a frightened look on his face.

"Release the speed lever," I yelled back. I ran alongside and pointed at the lever.

He got it under control, slowed down, and then turned a corner back into the living area. A lamp stand loomed directly in front of him. He didn't avoid it and hit it straight on. I caught the lamp just before it hit the floor. In his panic, he squeezed the reverse handle and backed into a television set. He bumped into a sofa, turned again and knocked over two standing plant stands and finally hit his own ash tray on the table scattering the ashes on the floor before coming to a complete stop.

Pop tried to regain his composure. Beads of sweat formed on his forehead and his hands were trembling. He had a look of disgust on his face. "I told you it was a stupid idea," he said.

Pop's stubbornness eventually won out. Despite loads of encouragement and support from me and the staff, he refused to master the motorized scooter. I knew he was capable. He refused to learn. Part of his refusal, I came to recognize, was because the idea was not his own. His concept of independence included the ability to determine his own solutions to his problems. Despite that he was insistent that I find an answer to his dilemma, he was actually venting his frustration rather than seeking an answer.

How people cope, assess, and deal with changing circumstances provides a hint to their spiritual awareness. Accepting one's limitations and being open to new directions is an indication of spiritual wholeness. It has been said that when people with strong spirituality meet situations of great challenge, the abstractions of spirituality become the concreteness of coping strategies. As I reflected upon Pop's attitude toward utilizing coping mechanisms, I realized he either was unaware of these resources or I failed to remind him.

Reading Glasses

"I need a new pair of glasses, Peter," Pop exclaimed to me the minute I arrived for a regular Wednesday visit. "I can't read with these anymore." He tore the glasses he was wearing from his face and dropped them onto the table beside him. They slid off the table and onto the floor. I picked them up and held them in my hands.

I looked closely at his glasses. No wonder he couldn't see. His glasses were severely scratched and covered with an inky film. He hardly ever cleaned them and when he did, he used the same handkerchief he used to blow his nose. I used a Kleenex from the box on the table to clean them and gave them back to him.

"That's a little better, but I still can't read very good with these," he said.

I never knew my father to be an avid reader. While growing up, I only remember him reading the daily Newark Evening News. It took time to read for pleasure and Pop claimed he never had time, what with his business, three kids always wanting something, and a wife with high maintenance. Reading was a leisure activity; something you did when you had nothing significant to do. I think that attitude was nurtured as a result of his watching Mom do a lot of reading when he thought she ought to be doing housework. Not reading was Pop's silent, passive aggressive protest against Moms overindulgence in reading.

Now, as he approached his eighties, Pop didn't find much pleasure in many activities beside reading. Reading became his passion; his sole preoccupation, and his escape. Reading was a diversion from Mom. An open newspaper in front of him served as an impenetrable barrier between himself and Mom and the rest of the outside world. Mom learned not to impinge upon this isolation.

Morning was Pop's newspaper reading time. He sat in the front room of the nursing home devouring every paper available. He read the news section, the sports section, the gardening section as well as the comics, healthy living, business, and obituaries. After lunch, he preferred magazines. He gravitated toward those that brought back memories - Yankee Magazine, Vermont Life, and New England Outdoors. A look of nostalgia came upon him as he read or glanced at pictures of quaint New England country life. He never abandoned his dream of the perfect retirement existence. If he could no longer expect to live the dream, he could still read about it.

Pop's "in-depth" reading consisted of Reader's Digest, Life Magazine, and National Geographic. He still expressed excitement, albeit somewhat subdued, when he read about a discovery of some ancient city, or how people cheated on their income taxes, or new information about Charles Lindbergh. Reading gave Pop vicarious pleasure. It kept him in touch with the world as he knew it, the world he missed, the world of his memories.

"My eyes get so damn tired," he repeated. "Things get blurry when I read. But I know what's wrong."

"You do," I responded. "And what do you think is wrong?"

"I need a new pair of reading glasses. You know, the kind you get at a pharmacy or department store." My father bought all his glasses at Woolworth's and claimed he never had any problems.

I knew his problem wasn't that simple to remedy. His last eye examination indicated that cataracts were forming in both eyes. It took pleading and promising and reminding him of his own words - "reading is my life" – to convince him to have the cataract operation. At first his sight improved. He was pleased. Soon afterward, however, it deteriorated until he felt slight pain and difficulty focusing.

"Damn butcher," he exclaimed when I would ask about his eyes.

"What do you mean," I asked.

"All I needed was a new pair of reading glasses. You could have gotten them at any drug store. But no, you had to take me to that butcher who screwed up my eyes even worse."

"Sometimes it's not the doctor's fault," I told him. "That kind of procedure may not last long. It's different with each person. Don't you remember the doctor telling you about the risks?"

Pop was not easily appeased.

"So what do you know? Are you a doctor now?" he said.

He had me there. There was no convincing him that the doctor was competent.

"They can do laser surgery," I suggested to him. "You remember the doctor telling you that if you needed it, he could do laser surgery that would restore some of your vision?"

"What the hell is laser surgery?" he asked. He thought for a moment and then added, "I'm not letting no eye butcher get near me again. I'm too old for some quack doctor to fool around with my eyes. Just take me to Woolworth's and I can find a pair of glasses that work."

"There are no Woolworth's anymore, Pop." I told him.

I don't think he believed me. He clucked his tongue in disgust and walked away.

Pop continued to read, but not without difficulty and not without complaints. To lose his sight would have been a cruel hoax, an insurmountable obstacle to living his last days. It wasn't my fault; I couldn't fix it, but I still felt responsible.

There may be two distinct approaches to viewing life, both of which hold value, but only one of which is intuitive. For my father, his focus was on the materialistic approach. He relied primarily upon his five senses – hearing, tasting, seeing, touching and smelling – to measure satisfaction in life. Whatever may be wrong with his personal life demanded a change in location or change in one or more materialistic attributes. His focus was on external changes to satisfy inner desires.

A second approach, the spiritual approach enables the person to see beyond the materialistic to an intuitive perspective. The person with a spiritual approach to life's dilemmas can look within for resources to cope with that which can't be changed on the outside. The spiritual dimension would have allowed my father the ability to find contentment despite any loss to the five senses.

Nothing challenges healthy spirituality more than unresolved guilt and remorse. Past experiences for which a person feels shame or regret, real or imaginary, can be so severe as to cause the person great anxiousness and character instability. Guilt affects the human psyche negatively, it saps one's mental energy, and frazzles the soul. It wears you down. There is the feeling of pending implosion if relief is not remedied.

Confession is also a spiritual experience, a "letting go," freeing one's self from transgressions that overwhelm one's mental stability. Confession is the release from guilt. Like its sister forgiveness, we don't know why it works, only that it does.

I can't say that I encouraged confessions or expressions of feelings from my parents. In our family, it was expected that emotions remain veiled. We knew of their presence, but avoided any outward displays. Feelings were kept to one's self unless it was anger or disappointment, neither of which I particularly wanted to awaken in my parents. What I didn't know wouldn't hurt me, and I was intent upon not getting hurt emotionally. Intimacy, a corollary of confession, spawns vulnerability and promotes disappointment. I discouraged confessions. But I soon found that I wasn't immune to what I couldn't control.

Private Conversations

"Peter, I have to talk to you privately," Pop announced as I arrived for a regular visit. He elongated the word "privately" to give it emphasis.

My father was hovering near the front door as if he was expecting me. For the past few weeks, each time I visited he tried to lure me aside, into a private room or an empty parlor, some place away from Mom. He used the pretense he had something very important he wanted to tell me. He needed privacy to talk. I had learned from experience that this usually meant listening to another litany of complaints about Mom.

I expected he would tell me "She keeps asking for cigarettes" or "She bumps into me with her chair and it's embarrassing," or "Peter you need to do something about her." He never was explicit. He didn't state something specific; it always sounded ambiguous and vague, innuendoes and insinuations. I needed something precise to which I could respond appropriately. So far I had successfully avoided his insistences.

"Peter, I need to talk with you privately," he persisted.

The word "privately" was my clue that he wanted to tell me something I probably didn't want to hear. When he talked "privately" it was never good news. It bordered on the personal, the confidential, the confessional or the intimate. Avoidance was my best defense. I dodged these conversations with great finesse. Today Pop seemed more insistent.

"Peter, we need to talk now."

"We can talk the next time I come up," I responded. "I can't stay long today. I need to get back to work."

I often used this diversionary tactic when attempting to evade any experience that hinted of intimacy. I don't know why I feared these invitations since rationally I knew they were Pop's attempt to confide in me as a trusted son, or his longing to come to terms with things that greatly bothered him or to find some sense of closure to a life he felt slowly withering away. They hinted of his spirituality. I clearly supported his justification for finding meaning and significance; it was his search for spirituality whether he was aware of this or not. My emotional fears, however, always trumped my rational thinking.

I tried to change the subject by physically pushing his wheelchair toward the front door and outside to the deck where other people were gathered. While among residents, he avoided personal conversations. This time, however, he could not be dissuaded. His hands gripped the wheels of his chair and abruptly brought it to a stop.

"I want to talk with you now," he told me. "I have something I need to get off my chest. Please can we go back to my room?"

He was more insistent than I anticipated. I feared the worst but felt trapped. I saw no options but to oblige him and accept whatever the circumstances demanded. I pushed him in his wheel chair down the hall toward his room. We didn't speak during the short trip.

"Okay Pop, what's on your mind?" I asked as I sat on his bed. Because of the timbre of reluctance in his voice and the aggrieved expression on his face, I suspected he was about to tell me something that pained him greatly, more than the usual litany of complaints about Mom.

Anticipating a request, I added, "I'll see what I can do," even before he began to talk. It was a spontaneous response when I sensed a request from him to be rescued from something.

That's how I saw myself, a fixer of problems, a rescuer from potential disaster, but hardly an active listener. I balked at allowing him to share a significant emotional moment. Despite my encouraging his spirituality, his insistence scared me.

Pop started to talk, slowly and hesitantly. "I don't know if I should tell you this."

He paused for a moment. Tears welled up in his eyes. Silence seemed to be the appropriate response for me at this moment. I sensed something was on his mind besides discontent with life in general. I did a mental search for a quick retort that might change the subject to avoid my having an emotional connection. Pop was about to let go of something. He didn't need encouraging. I sat silent fingering the crease of my pants.

"It's been on my mind for a long time." he said.

I sat silently.

"I really shouldn't tell you this, but after fifty years it's about time I do."

Again, my silence.

I neither encouraged nor discouraged him from continuing. I felt it was about to get uncomfortable, verging on the intimate, but knew I couldn't interrupt. He needed to get some matter off his chest. Today it felt appropriate to allow him to speak. I sensed something was very much amiss. I didn't want to hear his secrets, but I felt this time that offering the opportunity to clear his conscious was more important than my uncomfortable feeling. I would endure. It was a breakthrough for me that for once I recognized what was important to Pop. It was worth my taking time to hear.

"When your mother was younger," he continued, "she was very promiscuous. I don't mean she was a bad person or anything like that. She just liked to make friends with other men. Now this is the hard part." Again I noticed a slight wisp of tears in his eyes. "I am not your father. Another man is your father."

He stopped talking for a moment. I sat absolutely still, stunned, and silent. My eyes shifted from his face to my feet.

Pop continued. "One time before you were born, I was digging in the garden and accidentally poked my eye with the tip of a branch. My eye needed to be covered for three months. It was during that time that I suspect that your mother slept with this other man. I never met him, but I suspected who he was. Once when I went to visit your mother in the hospital when you were born, I saw him getting into a car and driving away."

I was dumbfounded. I could muster no words in response. I sat looking at my feet.

"I never really talked with your mother about this, but she knows that I know," Pop continued.

That didn't surprise me since I have embraced the family tradition of avoiding confrontation at all costs – it's always too risky.

"This has been on my mind for nearly fifty years, but I never wanted to tell you. I was afraid you wouldn't understand or get mad at me or blame your mother. I hope you won't be mad at me now."

Pop's demeanor suddenly went from remorse to conciliatory. He spoke with more fervor.

"I have appreciated how you have helped your mother and me these past few years. I hope this won't ruin our good relation. I have treated your mother and you as best as I was able despite that I am not your father. I'm sorry I had to tell you this but it's been bothering me for so long that it began to hurt."

I was feeling exhaustion and confusion as if I had run a marathon but couldn't find the finish line. I felt weary and lost. It crossed my mind briefly that it was all a fairy tale, an exaggeration made up to garner my sympathy. Pop just made up a whopper of a tale.

"You're not mad at me, are you," he asked? I remained silent. Then he asked again. "Are you mad at me? "

"No, I am not mad," I answered. "Don't worry about it."

My thoughts were no longer about my bewilderment, but rather about his security. I immediately sensed Pop was scared that I would abandon him or Mom or both, that I would not bring them cigarettes or candy or night time Excedrin. I realized Pop wanted to be reassured. Keeping his anxiety under control was very important, both to him and to me.

"Will you still help your mother and me," he asked? "Can you bring up some more cigarettes tomorrow?"

I reassured him that nothing would change. I would be back soon, and I would bring the stuff he wanted.

I left him and headed to my car wondering if what I had heard was true or pure fantasy. Did it really matter? How much did it matter? I kept wondering if he had read some magazine article or viewed some television show – Dr. Phil perhaps – about people who reveal hidden secrets as a way of seeking closure in life. Pop didn't have any secrets so he invented one that he might experience the closure that comes with its revelation. Or was he seeking attention, one more way of manipulating me to test my love and affection? It felt very bizarre as if part of a television soap opera. Should I be prepared for more intimate revelations he might share?

Pop's confession seemed to come out of the blue. I searched for a reason but could find no particular circumstance – no knowledge of a new devastating sickness, no new broken relationship, no sudden awareness of impending death – that would precipitate it. I couldn't tell if it was the truth, but was beginning to recognize that the truth was not what mattered.

I didn't think I wanted to know the truth. I felt no compulsion to make any changes in our relationship whether true or not. I wanted to let the story, the situation, the knowledge drift away; to let it go, to make no difference. My sense of responsibility for my parents would not change. My concern seemed more focused on knowing I was a reliable person who was willing to assume a mature, trustworthy, and culpable position as caretaker for my parents. How I evaluated myself in this regard was equally as important as my attitude toward my parents.

Still, I wondered what prompted Pop to reveal this secret to me. What need did it fulfill for him? I am sure it must have been painful for him to conjure up this story that he wasn't my father. He could have kept the secret, avoided any pain, and I would never have known. What purpose was served in my knowing? I had no inkling that he wanted to hurt me or seek revenge for some misdeed I might have committed toward him many years ago.

As I pondered this situation the many months afterward, I came to realize that a person anticipating the last throws of life seeks diligently to set the record straight, to rid themselves of any lingering doubts or fears of unsettled business. For my father, I think it was an exercise in self therapy, a means for facilitating healing or seeking a sense of wholeness. It called into question his understanding of spirituality as that emerging feeling of seeking what is significant in one's life. People in the later stages of life often find the need, but not always the opportunity, to come to terms with their sometimes discretions in their past. This was Pop's opportunity. I was glad he trusted me with his secrets and felt comfortable that I would not betray him or ignore him or belittle him.

Pop was not religious, so I doubted it was his attempt to come clean with God. But that didn't mean he was without spirituality. He embraced principals for maintaining morals in life. He retained the need for structure and meaning and sought to explore it. His spirituality in this circumstance provided a framework for managing concerns and decisions toward the end of his time. It must have been this seeking for wholeness in life that prompted him to accept the pain and the consequences of admitting to a long held secret.

I eventually recognized my own failures in responding to this incident. Overwhelmed by my own fears of becoming involved in something far too intimate to be comfortable, I was not able to pursue the circumstances for the benefit of Pop. I could have offered him the opportunity to explore further the reason for his revelation to me at this time. It's hard to conclude that wanting me to know his secret was his only motivation for confiding in me. If he saw me as a trusted son and felt comfortable talking with me about such personal matters, it surely met some needs beyond clearing one particular secret. I too easily dismissed the opportunity to allow Pop some sense of achieving wholeness in spirit because of my own fears of the consequences of his sharing something intimate with me. The lesson for me was that I needed to address my own fears if I were ever to be the channel through which my parents were able to face their fears – fears of the aging process stealing their years and life before they achieved completeness.

The nature of spirituality may differ under dissimilar circumstances, but it always encourages the person to seek after what holds meaning and significance in life regardless of one's age or health or status. There are those times and circumstances when spirituality is triggered by the most unlikely circumstances.

4

Growing Old Gracefully or Checking Out Easily

Said the little boy, "Sometimes I drop my spoon."
Said the old man, "I do that too."
The little boy whispered, "I wet my pants."
"I do that too," laughed the old man.
Said the little boy, "I often cry."
The old man nodded, "So do I."
"But worst of all," said the boy, "it seems
grown-ups don't pay attention to me."
And he felt the warmth of a wrinkled old hand.
"I know what you mean," said the old man.
...Shel Silverstein.

There comes a time in the age and stage of adulthood when the person begins to focus on the end. Recognition of the future looks bleak. The reality that there may be no future becomes a real possibility. I suspect this awareness comes at different times for different people but eventually it does come for everyone.

I began to recognize this awareness in my father from listening to him as he expressed a growing consciousness of the possibility of death. He didn't avoid the subject completely. He provided hints that he was beginning to come to terms with it. His increased conversation about the means of dying was my first recognition that the subject was constantly on his mind. He didn't hesitate to talk about methods of his own death but hesitated to raise questions he might have had about the meaning of his death.

Reflections at Ninety

We decided to celebrate Pop's ninetieth birthday. More correctly, his family decided to celebrate his birthday despite Pop. He wasn't excited. My brothers came for the week-end. A grandson came from Florida and brought Pop's first great grandchild. I ordered a special cake and invited some of his favorite staff. A room was designated as the "party room" at the home and colored streamers and balloons were placed in appropriate positions to give a feeling of celebration.

I read that age and stage of life celebrations, especially for older people, becomes a foundation for maintaining a healthy spirituality. These celebrations help re-connect with family, foster fond recollections, and focus on the significance of the person, all of which nurture the soul.

Pop wasn't enthusiastic about any party. He seemed more anxious than expectant.

"They are coming after lunch, right?" Pop asked. "I can't sit around very long. And they will need to be gone before supper."

Pop tried to justify his anxiousness. "I can't take much noise you know. It makes me nervous." He doesn't mention kids, but I knew how uptight he got around kids. The slightest sudden squeal or spontaneous holler uttered from a high pitched child's voice sent Pop wincing. His face would curl up in pain and he clenched his fits. Noise and confusion have always caused him grief no matter what his age. He was particularly sensitive now.

I think his anxiety this day was more a reaction to a disruption in his routine. At the nursing home he settled into a daily regimen. Things happened in sequence and at specific times. That's how Pop liked it. He didn't say so but I imagined it gave him security. Everything has a time and a time for everything brought order to his world. Disruption to this routine caused him, great consternation. I think he was afraid the party would cause disruption from which he wouldn't recover.

"I need to have my supper at 5:30 and I want to watch the news at 6:00," he reminds me.

At three o'clock, we had the sun room ready for his party. My brothers arrived and his first great grandson looked curiously at great grandpa. Neither of them seemed anxious to make contact. The long table was decorated with a colorful paper table cloth. Plastic plates and spoons were in a pile in the middle of the table. A cake was on one end and two half gallons of ice cream, one coffee and one vanilla, were slowly melting on the other end. Mom was in her wheelchair almost panting. She couldn't wait to get some ice cream. She reached for a bowl and we had to restrain her. Her great grandson was being refrained from sticking his fingers in the icing on the cake. Pop sat at the head of the table with a funny hat on his head that he kept taking off and putting back on as if he forgot it was there or wished it weren't. He didn't look joyful.

Despite that he lived in the home for nearly five years and another three years next door in the assisted living facility, he had no resident friends. None were present for the party. Instead, he insisted that we ask a few of his favorite nurses, nurse aides, and cleaning ladies. It felt awkward to invite staff as if they were paid to be present. Did they come because they were paid or out of respect or for a few minutes relief from their duties?

Pop was a friendly guy and open, if not willing, to meet new people. But not now. He claimed that the other residents in the nursing facility were all from Texas. They are unimpressed by his East Coast experience. When he initiated conversation, all they talked about was Texas. He's wasn't interested or perhaps a bit annoyed to be always talking about Texas, so he didn't talk at all and stayed to himself. This drastic change in attitude did not bode well for his ability to be part of a community. It was the reason no other residents were present for his party

Pop was never a loner and his withdrawal from socialization caused me concern. I thought he needed to be surrounded and supported by a community otherwise he would continue feeling aloof and separated. Loneliness in the midst of a crowd must be an awful feeling to endure. I thought about this but was not able to remedy the situation.

The party went well. Mom ate ice cream until she complained that her stomach hurt. Her favorite was coffee flavored and her dress was awash in coffee colored spots. The grandson was complacent licking icing off each person's piece of cake. Despite being sugar coated and sugar fueled, not a peep came from his mouth. He was content.

After one hour, Pop asked to go back to his room.

"I'm getting tired," he states. "Too much excitement."

I think he was still anxious about his routine and wanted to be sure nothing interrupted his expectations. With some disappointment that he was not as excited as I had hoped about turning ninety and celebrating with his family, I escorted Pop back to his room. The party crashed soon after all the food is gone.

Pop was now into his ninety-first year, four years older than when his own father died. He talked about being ready to die, but it's hard to tell if that's because his limited abilities made his life extremely boring or all the challenges of daily living had become giant annoyances to him or he just felt plain worn out. He told me that his father, when he decided that he lived long enough, simply went to bed and never got up again. I sensed that Pop told me this because he thought about doing the same thing.

I thought about Pop's life. He had achieved quantity, but I am not sure about the quality. I thought he would agree with me. I often heard his persistent anxieties and displeasures. "Life stinks," he often reminded me.

Pop claimed he had lived long enough, but he didn't talk much about whether he had lived well enough. He told me he no longer wanted to live, but lamented that he was too healthy to die. He confronted the same dilemma I imagined so many aging people must face, achieving a balance between quantity and quality of life.

Pop didn't seem to fear death. He talked about death as if it was an escape from this life, but I wondered if he thought of death as moving into a new life. We hadn't talked about this. I didn't know how he felt about a "new life" after death.

I was reminded of the biblical perspective of life as a time of "just passing through."

I thought Pop interpreted the idea of "just passing through" as fatalistic, that life was temporary, and death was final and ultimate. I understood his contention that if he couldn't do things the way he had always done them then he didn't want to do them at all. It made sense to him. He became discouraged. He wanted to give up. Life became unbearable, and he thought it was best to just drop out. But he's not expressed any curiosity about the meaning of death or about life after death.

My mistake was to never ask him to talk to me about death. Perhaps if I pressed him gently, encouraged him to share his feelings, hearing himself talk might have brought clarity to his perspective and peacefulness to his decisions. Open conversation about one's problems or dilemmas often allows the person to see these problems in a new perspective, attain a better understanding, and lose any fears attached. It allows a person to "let go."

Christian spirituality promotes the idea that death is never in vain. It has meaning and significance. Death is not the end of life; it is a part of life. I never broached this idea with Pop; never invited him to tell me about his feelings, his fears, or perhaps his anticipation about life after death. At his age, it must have been on his mind. I think now it would have been a great relief for him to talk about his own death. Even if he raised questions we couldn't answer, just the conversation would have helped his acceptance. Our spirituality may not always provide resolutions, but it mandates that we confront those significant issues head on.

Is there a relationship between the physical and the spiritual? There was a time when most professionals acknowledged that no relationship existed. The physical could be seen, touched, felt, x-rayed, measured, and analyzed. The spiritual was intangible, beyond knowing, only conjecture. This assumes a limited and deficient understanding of the role of spirituality. Spirituality plays a large part in controlling a person's attitudes and behaviors.

. . . .

No one lives forever. I imagined the day when death would overtake my parents. This thought didn't consume my mind daily, but crept into my thinking periodically.

As they grew older and daily living became more and more of a challenge for them, I do admit that there were times when I wished that death would come sooner rather than later. Watching them slowly deteriorate was difficult for me, especially when I realized that there was little I could do to improve their condition. I often thought it not a tragedy but a welcome release for them as well as for me if death were to happen. No longer would they "suffer" real or imagined experiences. Their daily life was a struggle from wake up time to bed time.

Pop, especially, entertained these end of life thoughts. What spirituality he communicated to me focused those last few years not on growing old gracefully with a heartfelt recollection of a life well spent, but rather how he could check out easily, get death over with as simply as possible. More than once he broached the subject of death with me. He wasn't curious. He didn't wonder about life in the hereafter or how it might be meaningful. He didn't express thoughts of putting his affairs in order. He didn't want to make amends for past occurrences or seek forgiveness. The ethereal of death didn't appear to concern him. He focused his attention how to end his life with as little effort and pain as possible. He even asked once if I could get him a gun.

Pop refused to explore the meaning of dying or death. I hesitated to broach the subject for fear of instigating ideas he might not want to discuss. The subject was simply not discussed with any seriousness outside of how best to die. What understanding he had about his impending death I could only glean from hints he provided, from his level of dissatisfaction and the seriousness of his discontent, from his remarks about potential suicide, from his inability to seek coping mechanism, and from slices of conversations he offered about maintaining relationships.

What If...

"How are you doing, Pop? I asked my father as I arrived for a regular visit. That was a major mistake. I opened myself to a litany of his complaints, troubles, and discontentment's.

"Terrible," he replied. "My eyes. I can't see anything anymore. It hurts to read. What's going to happen, Peter, if I can't read anymore? Reading is my only enjoyment."

I reminded him that the eye doctor told him he wasn't going blind.

"Your sight might be changing somewhat, but losing it altogether isn't going too happen," I said. Pop was not consoled. We had had this conversation in one form or another many times. His solution then was new reading glasses, but had now given this up as a real solution.

"And my legs. They hurt bad. I can hardly walk," he continued.

A grimaced look of anguish came over his face as he reflected on what he just told me. I had grown used to this look. It was one of despair. He exposed it each time he talked about his future and how dim it seemed to be.

"What if I can't get around, Peter? What happens then?"

Pop had great difficulty accepting change. All change, he reasoned, no matter how slight, was abhorrent. He detested it. Change shouldn't happen. It only disrupts your life. Change, he confided, only presented a challenge that couldn't be met. He had resigned himself a few years back that if he could not do things they way he had always done them; he wouldn't do them at all. Coping skills were not his best suit. Any suggestions from me about improving his circumstances were greeted with distain. He didn't want a remote control for the television. A scooter to assist him with walking was out of the question. Laser surgery to correct his vision was maligned. Each was a possibility, but only with his cooperation and approval. He neither wanted to cooperate or approve

"I can get you a remote control. You can remain in your chair when you want to change channels," I told him

"Too damn hard to learn now," he replied.

"How about bifocals so you can read more easily?" I asked

He voted that down.

"I can make an appointment with the dentist. I'm sure he can do something about the ache you say you have in your gums," I added.

"These new dentists just want to make more money. They don't do any good," was his response. His teeth stayed rotten

He made the decision he had no future; his only option was to endure until the end came. Despite not being a happy camper, Pop wanted things to stay the same. His routine was his only salvation.

Pop was a pessimist to the umpteenth degree. Pending catastrophes loomed ever nearby. "What will I do if…?" summed up his attitude about all things possible and impossible. Every suggestion about resolving a predicament, a problem, a possibility for change was met with a counterargument. "What will I do if…?"

Pop figured the future would most likely not be better, only worse. This realization was the source of his depression and extreme anxiety. It nurtured his desire to want to check out of life rather than engage it. No amount of "it will be okay, Pop," or "don't worry so much" had any effect or relieving his consternation or providing much consolation. I stopped this approach knowing that I was addressing a possibility not a reality.

I learned that trying to resolve his many problems was futile. He liked being discontent. Most times, he didn't want a resolution; he just wanted to be heard. Solving problems meant accepting changes. He didn't like changes. What he really wanted was a chance to vent his fears and be heard. I suspected that Pop was well aware of the consequences of the aging process, that growing older was not growing better, and that the unwanted ramifications just came with the territory. He could live with that. What he found intolerable was having no one with whom he could share his fears.

Sharing of fears is an intricate part of plugging into one's spiritual side. Recognizing one's weaknesses and articulating them is a form of release that only comes from taping into spirituality.

"I'm Sorry I Have To Go This Way"

Pop often talked openly about suicide. He was not overly emotional. The subject of suicide elicited the same emotions as if talking about the weather. He seemed comfortable with the idea. His perspective about suicide was the same as his perspective on growing flowers. When they needed pruning, you just cut them down. It was a natural thing to do.

He told me he wanted to die; he was ready to die. He wasn't afraid of dying. He wasn't just kidding. It was not a ploy to get attention. He didn't want to explore the idea of meaning in death or concerns about afterlife; he just wanted to die and get it over with. I gleaned this understanding from the frank way by which he registered his disillusionment about continuing to live.

"One day my father decided he wasn't going to get up anymore," Pop told me. "He was going to stay in bed, stop eating, and lay there until he died. I think I will do the same thing."

Suicide happened in our family before. It was no stranger. My grandfather on my mother's side took his shot gun into the closet with him, placed the barrel of the loaded gun inside his mouth, rigged the trigger to the door handle, and slammed the door shut. He had been suffering from some debilitating disease that curtailed his active lifestyle. Without his activity, he saw no reason to keep living. Pop's father's death – staying in bed until death came – was a passive suicide.

"I just want to die," Pop told me often. "I having nothing left to live for. I have no friends. I don't like living here in Texas. My legs hurt. My teeth are rotten. I can't take care of your mother. It's no use. I'm no use."

There was both desperation and solace in his voice. I said nothing but waited to see his reaction to his own thoughts. He waited to see mine. I was past the point of attempting to convince him there was still reason to live. If I mentioned he needed to see his future great grandchildren, he wasn't impressed. If I suggested he hang on until after other grandchildren graduated, he sloughed it off as unimportant.

"Mom needs you," I told him.

"The home will take care of her," he responded.

"Christmas and Thanksgiving just won't be the same without you," I told him.

The thought occurred that perhaps his focus on dying was a ploy. He was manipulating me to get attention. He was depressed. I rationalized that it must be his realization of limited time left that caused depression. Depression is often accompanied by thoughts of suicide. I didn't blame him for feeling this way. If death was his focus, why would I try to talk him out of it, especially at his age? At the very least, he deserved to be heard. An attentive ear and an understanding audience might not change the inevitable but it could help alleviate his emotional anguish. Besides, I had learned that he didn't want me to intervene; he only wanted me to listen.

I didn't fear his dying. I did fear how he might die. Dying in his sleep or as the consequence of a heart attack or stroke or simply from old age was normal. But suicide felt different. I was afraid he might not be able to handle suicide. I was afraid he might botch it; that he would try it but not succeed and be worse off than he was now. Maybe the suicide attempt would leave him brain dead or in a coma from which he would suffer a long time. I also felt that his attempt at suicide would reflect on me, that it proved I was incapable as a care taker. I would be at fault for neglect. I hoped for a quick death by natural causes.

Pop continued to talk about lying in bed until he died like his father. This sounded too much like an agonizing and painfully slow process of increasing malnutrition and bedsores. That had to be averted. I shuddered at the thought.

"Peter, can you get me a gun? He asked. The question took me by surprise. He asked as if assuming I owned a gun.

"No, I can't Pop," I answered. As I thought about his request for a gun, I considered it a more humane way than lying in bed until death comes. Still I could not bring myself to assist him in this endeavor.

The phone rang early one morning at my house.

"There has been some kind of an accident with your father," the voice at the other end announced.

"What kind of an accident," I asked? "Is he alright?"

"I think so," she said. "It looks like he fell sometime during the night and bumped his head, maybe a concussion, and couldn't get up. We found him lying on the floor but you need to come up. We called EMS and they are on their way. Can you come now?"

I told her I would be right there. It would take about fifteen minutes.

When I arrived, they filled me in with details. The paper delivery lady had been knocking on Pop's door persistently with no response. She became suspicious when Pop failed to pick up his paper as he usually did early each morning. It remained on the floor outside his door when she passed by an hour later. Every one in the complex knew his routine. It was too late for him to be sleeping.

This morning no one had seen him. The decision was made to check on Pop. With a passkey, the staff opened his door and found him lying on the floor. He appeared unconscious. They were able to awaken him but his speech was incoherent. He couldn't explain what happened. They immediately called EMS, and then called me.

I left the office and went directly to his room. The elevator ride up to the third floor was the slowest imaginable. When I entered the room I saw two EMS personal as they knelt over Pop. I couldn't see Pop's face. I moved around toward his head. He saw me. His eyes looked hazy. I told him I was there but he did not respond. I watched them strap him onto a gurney and brace his head with a belt. Again, I spoke to him. He was awake and mumbled incoherently. I could only make out a few words.

"Peter, I'm sorry for causing you this trouble."

"Don't worry about it now," I told him.

The EMS workers were anxious to get him to the hospital.

"They're taking you to the hospital," I said. "I'll go there with you."

They carried him out the door, down the elevator, and into a waiting ambulance. The nearest hospital was only minutes away.

I glanced around the apartment, looking for anything he might need at the hospital. I noticed an envelope lying on a bedside table. It was addressed to me. I ripped it open and began to read.

"Dear Peter," it began. "I am sorry that I have to go this way, but it's the best way. I can't take the pain anymore. My legs hurt too much. Don't tell anybody what happen, not even your mother. I will be ok. Love Pop."

On the floor under the table was an empty medicine bottle. I read the label. It once held prescription sleeping tablets, but no more. I shoved the note and the bottle in my pocket and left for the hospital.

Pop had regained his composure shortly after reaching the hospital. He was talkative now and coherent, even joking with the nurses in the emergency room. When I asked him to tell me specifics about what he had done, he was evasive.

"I sure took me a snooze," he said. "I was out like a light. I don't remember much. I hope I didn't cause you much trouble, Peter."

It was difficult to tell if he was really conscious of what had happened or that he felt embarrassed and wished to avoid the subject.

I pressed him.

"Pop, why did you take all those pills," I asked?

He hesitated to answer. He looked around the room as if to see if anyone else heard my question.

"I don't want to talk about that now," he said.

I let the interrogation drop for the time being but planned to pursue it further as he recovered. The first consideration was to determine the lasting effects from the overdose.

"Did he take enough pills to do him much harm," I asked the doctor.

"More than enough to kill an average healthy young man," he responded. He shook his head as if in disbelief that Pop wasn't dead.

Pop remained in the hospital a few days. Despite his stated antipathy about hospitals, he loved the attention – food prepared and served in his room, a newspaper each morning, pretty nurses checking his temperature and bedsores, naps whenever he wanted, the six o'clock news, and Mom not asking for cigarettes constantly.

I was confident the note was about attempted suicide, but failed to mention it while he was in the hospital. I was afraid to broach the subject. The thought of suicide so upset me that I got angry thinking about it. It would be best to ignore it and save him the embarrassment of admitting his failure. I felt that bringing up the subject might just cause emotional stress. Unfortunately I always tried to avoid unpleasant conversations.

The nursing home administration found out about the note from the apartment staff and required certain stipulations before he could move back to the home. He had to be "certified as sane" by a consulting psychologist. Pop disliked shrinks. Despite his non-cooperation, he was nevertheless readmitted.

Pop decide to tell Mom about his suicide. He didn't choose a sensitive manner to communicate this but rather bluntly blurted it out and told her he didn't want to live anymore. Mom was confused but still rational enough then to comprehend him. It frightened her tremendously in her disturbed condition.

"I don't like him talking crazy like that," she said. She started to cry which I hadn't observed for many years.

I asked Pop to cease and desist his talk about dying in front of Mom; that it disturbed her tremendously and only served to deepen her dementia. I didn't know this factually, but it was an attempt to save Mom from painful thoughts. Her state of mind just couldn't deal with trauma. Still Pop continued to drop hints in front of her about wanting to die. I thought it just a matter of time before he tried suicide again.

Pop Died Last night

Pop died last night. Actually he died two weeks ago. He lay in bed and refused to eat, refused to get up, refused to read, refused to talk, refused to do anything but lie there in silence. He breathed all that time; only stopping last night.

A month ago, true to his word, he went to bed and refused to get up the next day. We coaxed him and coaxed him, encouraged him to get up, told him it was a silly way to die, and even got angry at his behavior. He refused to budge. He said he was going to stay there until he died.

For the first week, he continued his routine from bed. He watched television, read the morning paper, had his meals delivered to his room, made a few phone calls, and allowed me to visit. He expressed agitation at the screamers; the residents on his floor who shouted loudly and incoherently both day and night. Noise pollution, he called it. Beside these few diversions, he slept most of the time.

Despite herculean efforts from staff and me, he could not be convinced to get out of bed.

"Enough is enough," he said.

Soon he stopped complaining about the screamers. He stopped caring if his paper was delivered. He didn't want to smoke. He asked for nothing, wanted to do nothing, wanted no food, and slept all the time.

Pop was in total control. He made the conscious decision that he "couldn't take it any more." Impassioned by his desire to "get out of this" he saw his life as no longer necessary. After a few days of fruitless efforts to change his mind, I began to welcome death and the possibility of closure.

There was no medical emergency. The staff had accepted his decision. They were used to people dying at the home, albeit not under such circumstances. They expressed no undue concern. We didn't consult with doctors or resort to hospitalization. Treatment was not called for or necessary. He would have refused any intervention.

My concern was about pain. Would he begin to suffer from lack of food and water and become dehydrated? How long could he remain alive without any sustenance? Complications were bound to occur – pneumonia, internal bleeding, congestion and pain. How would he handle these? How would I handle these?

Pop had led an almost pain free existence for ninety years, at least physically. Any sicknesses or accidents he experienced were minor. I wondered if he was aware of what he might have to endure by just giving up and lying there in bed. Did he think he would just go to sleep peacefully? I could feel panic setting in. My anxiety felt overwhelming as I considered his limited options. I thought about how I would feel throughout this ordeal.

I contacted hospice. I knew their services focused on relieving pain for the dying. They agreed to serve as "manager" for his last days, no matter how many. I felt a great sense of relief as I trusted their ability and sensitivity to provide care. They bolstered my hopefulness and relieved my anxiety. Pop was in good hands. They administered various medications to keep him comfortable – Vicodan, morphine patches, and anti-congestion medications. Despite his rapid loss of weight, his lack of food, and his gaunt appearance, the pain management seemed to work well. I saw no grimacing on Pop's face.

My brothers came for a short visit. Pop responded with minimal nods and grunts. When they left, he shut down immediately. A few days later he could barely swallow. Medications had to be given intravenously. His breathing became halted and shallow. When I called his name, he didn't respond.

I began to grow tired of the long vigils of waiting and watching. There was nothing I could do to change the circumstances. I was terrified he might contract some new complication that would increase his agony, and mine. He was resting comfortably and I wished for a quick death. No more anxiety, no more worry, no more discontent. But it just seemed the end would never come.

I felt no compulsion to hear confessions nor did I attempt to offer Pop counsel. I was aware that reassuring words for those approaching death might provide some comfort, that death was never in vain or that he was headed for a better place or that it was alright for him to let go and let God, but I refrained from speaking. These were intimate thoughts and I was not used to sharing intimacy with Pop. I don't think he would have heard my voice. My primary consideration was, "Let's just get this death over with and then we can move on." I was not proud of these thoughts. I knew I could handle the grief once death was past.

Finally the end came. His breathing stopped. His heart stopped. Pop dozed off. He looked peaceful. My wife and I were at his bedside. A staff person folded his hands over his chest. His chin was propped up and his mouth held closed by a rolled up towel placed under his chin and against his upper chest. I thought it looked awkward and uncomfortable and I wanted to remove it. I bent down to pick the towel up when my wife said, "Leave it there or else his mouth will drop open and it will look like he is dying."

The chaplain offered us comfort by sharing the twenty-third psalm, the Lord's Prayer, and some related scripture "In my father's house are many dwellings places…And if I go and prepare a place for you, I will come again and will take you to myself, so that where I am, there you may be also" (NRSV, John 14, 2-3). The words helped with closure; at least it was a beginning. These words also helped me to accept Pop's death as not entirely in vain, not entirely unremarkable. I remember feeling a great sense of relief, not by his death as much by the release of his suffering. His suffering had become my suffering.

Like a rush of water that overcomes the beach front during high tide, my thoughts went immediately to my mother and to the overwhelming task of telling her Pop died. Even more than having to accept his death, I shuddered at the thought of telling Mom.

Closure

Pop died last night and now I had to tell Mom. Nobody had told her. The staff of the nursing home thought it best that I tell her. I feared doing this far more than I feared Pop dying.

I hesitated, thinking that her dementia might prevent her from fully comprehending what happened. I thought perhaps it best I not tell her for fear of confusing her. My wife said it would be cruel not to tell her. She deserved to know. They had been married sixty five years.

I recognized I was stalling. My apprehension got the better of my sense of responsibility. How would Mom respond? Would feelings of grief and despondency overwhelm her? Would she become uncontrollable? My fear of her reactions prompted my procrastination. These feelings consumed my thoughts as I approached the nursing home. My fear of the unknown was not a comfortable feeling.

Deep down, I hoped that she would respond in some manner. I wanted her to have feelings and emotions, signs that she still retained some semblance of humanness. If she expressed sadness and despondency at Pop's death, I rationalized, she then could also feel grief's healing power, it's cleansing activity, its ability to bring closure.

Mom sat in the front parlor. She was in her wheelchair close to the front door. I was reminded it was where she and Pop always sat right after breakfast while Pop read his newspaper and Mom pleaded for cigarettes. She looked forlorn and disconsolate, staring out the window. I wondered if another resident might have told her about Pop's dying. I sat down beside her and she greeted me with her toothless grin. I assumed she had lost her teeth again.

"Where are your teeth, Mom" I asked her?

"I don't know," she replied. Then she added, "I don't know what you are talking about."

We sat in silence for a few moments.

"Mom, Pop died last night," I told her.

She offered no response but looked at me intently as if contemplating what I was telling her. I had given her a cigarette and she took a long, labored drag, held her breath for a few seconds, and slowly and deliberately exhaled, blowing smoke between her pursed lips.

"He just fell asleep and didn't wake up. He died in his sleep peacefully," I added.

Still no response from Mom. She stared alternately at me and then out the window. We both sat silently. I interrupted the silence.

"What are you thinking, Mom," I asked her.

"About the old man," she replied.

"What old man? " I asked.

"The one that died last night," she said.

We sat in silence again. I wondered what impressions she retained from my telling her about Pop dying. She seemed to have some comprehension that someone died, but not necessarily someone she knew. I was prepared to offer comfort and solace, but the circumstances didn't require it. I was not sure what Mom had heard or how she was responding.

Mom sat in silence smoking her cigarette until it burned down nearly to her fingertips. I took it away and ground it out in the ash tray. She asked for another cigarette.

"What are you thinking about the old man that died last night?" I asked her.

"It makes me sad," she said.

Again we sat silently while Mom smiled at me, smoked her cigarette, and occasionally stared out the window.

"Tell me again about the old man that died last night," I asked again.

"What old man?" she replied.

"The one that died last night," I said. "Pop died last night. Don't you understand?"

"I don't know who you mean. What are you talking about?" she said. "Can I have another cigarette?"

At different times over the next few days and weeks, I would ask Mom what she was thinking. Did she remember the old man who died? Sometimes she replied that yes, she had been thinking about that old man but could recall nothing about who the old man was. Other times she had no recollection at all.

"I don't know what you are talking about."

Mom wanted another cigarette and then to go out for ice cream and candy. I obliged her willingly.

Living Alone

Nursing homes can be lonely. Despite that many other residents are constantly present, each person lives an isolated existence. I have met residents who have been roommates and still didn't know each other's names. Staff has to care about large numbers of residents so avoid becoming too friendly with any one person. When working with the old and frail there is always the threat of imminent death looming. The fear of loss is a powerful detriment for allowing one's self to become too attached.

Mom lived pretty much alone now. She had always been a dependent person. She experienced difficulty making decisions, fending for herself, and knowing how to respond to crisis. She was used to being taken care of - by her father, by Pop, by all sorts and kinds of medical people, and now by me. Her inclination toward independence was relinquished years ago.

Mom was not a person with great ambition. I did not remember her having a vibrant curiosity She relied heavily on others to unravel the mysteries of life. She attached herself, even became addicted, to whatever she found that relieved stress or tension or stomachache. Soothing discomfort and overcoming distress where the primary functions of pills to which Mom subscribed willingly. She used television and books as a means for withdrawal. Over the years when she considered life unbearable, she was known to retreat to her room and not come out for days. Isolation was a form of therapy for Mom. Whatever seemed to release pain – medications, withdrawal, alcohol, or feigned sickness – Mom clung to with a vengeance.

Mom relied heavily on Pop for security and stability in her life. He stood by her as she sought solace from one doctor to another, one treatment program to another, one medication to another. Despite that he thought her condition to be self-inflicted - that she was basically mentally unstable and her chosen life style was a contributing factor - he always held out hope that she might change. Her history suggested otherwise. Despite what progress Mom made, she quickly fell back into old routines and familiar patterns.

Mom's addiction to dependency was partially Pops fault. He was unwilling to allow Mom to suffer any consequences of her life-style choices. When she acted dysfunctional, he covered it up by pretending she was just having a bad day or had too much to drink the previous evening. He refused to face the truth of her mental fragility. Her actions did anger him when they would disrupt his routine or when he faced the embarrassment of explaining her to friends and family but he never acted on that anger.

Pop didn't spend much time or energy trying to "fix" Mom's circumstances. Instead he either ignored her or sulked in silence. His levels of anxiety and worry greatly magnified to the point of paralysis, but he couldn't bring himself to take specific action to remedy the situations. He dealt with his frustration by mumbling and seething under his breath.

Deep down, I believed Pop to be a compassionate man, but unable to express it openly. It must have been difficult for him to live with the erratic behavior of Mom. If he recognized what she really needed - to assume personal responsibility and face her own behavioral consequences - he still encouraged her co-dependency. He made excuses for her when she feigned sickness, denied acknowledging her need for professional treatment, and allowed her to blame other people and external forces for her own internal strife. Pop was resigned to his frustration.

Pop had died and now Mom was alone. The home had replaced Pop as her primary caretaker and she had transferred her dependency to the staff, both willingly and unwillingly. She ate well. She was kept clean. Her medications were monitored. She had her hair done once every two weeks. What more could a person want from life? I saw no reason to move her from the nursing home.

Still she was alone now. She lived the isolated nursing home existence. She acknowledged other residents but engaged in no personal conversations. Her only response to staff requests were "yes" and "no" or "Get the hell away from me".

Her dementia accelerated. Mom could barely complete a sentence. Her memory failed completely except for isolated glimpses of experiences far in the past. I wondered if she had any thoughts or feelings about her present life, about the family she once knew well, or about her past. Her affect was flat. Her responses to queries varied only slightly. "I can't remember," or "No, I don't hurt anyplace," or "I don't know what you are talking about."

It was difficult to connect with Mom. I refrained from treating her like a child although the temptation was great because of the symptoms of dementia. I had replaced my father in the role of caretaker for her, but I wanted to remain as aloof as possible so as not to encourage undue dependency. I was the only family she recognized and sometimes that was difficult for her. I felt in a quandary about my role in Mom's life now that Pop had died.

5

Mom's Melancholy

"The journey into dementia has its disappointments to be endured as well as its triumphs to be cherished. In all of the ambiguities and confusion there may also be signs of hope, for this is a journey with intersecting signposts; reminders of the past and pointers to the future. There arealways fresh opportunities for a new walk on a new day." ...Hudson, Rosalie, (2006) *"Spirited Walking"* in M. Marshal and K. Allan, Dementia: Walking not Wandering, London: Hawker, (p.113)

Dementia infiltrates every pore of the person it strikes. It sucks enjoyment from life. It causes routine tasks to become overwhelming obstacles. There is no denying that it radically alters how the person lives each day. Daily life becomes a constant struggle. Nothing appears to make sense. Just completing a thought or a sentence is a substantial challenge.

Dementia adds a new dimension to one's life. It greatly alters that person but also all those with whom that person comes in contact. One person's dementia demands a great deal of patience and grace from other family members to avoid the frustration that such radical behavioral change causes. It disrupts the entire family.

Mom's dementia certainly tried my patience. Sometimes the frustration simply overwhelmed me and I avoided visiting with her. Other times, I swallowed my self-absorption and attempted, to the best of my limited ability, to be as patient, tolerant, and graceful as possible. I truly wanted her to experience life as normally and as fully as might be possible under the circumstances.

Despite the dementia, daily life continued for Mom after Pop died. Each visit I made often brought a new experience with new challenges. I soon learned, with great humility, the depths of the effects of dementia on her behavior and personality. Her change in communication and mannerisms demanded new approaches to meeting her personal requirements. Sometimes the unexpected occurred. What I planned for the regular visit would invariably turn into a different experience altogether. I needed to be prepared and ready to make momentary adjustments. Comic relief was not intentional but occurred more often than I expected.

Following Pop's death, visiting with mom took on a new dimension. I felt she needed constant attention and reminding of who she was and visits that were routine and expected might serve this purpose best. I continued my visits with Mom almost every Wednesday afternoon as well as Sundays. Nothing proved to be routine about the visits. Despite that we often planned the same experiences – an afternoon shopping, a walk outside, a meal together at the home, or just sitting and smoking – unintended consequences often occurred from unexpected experiences. For those people who visit loved ones with dementia, be prepared. The unexpected is never to be ignored or very far away.

Afternoon Shopping

It wasn't often, but Mom could be very verbal and direct about what she wanted. The first words I heard when I arrived for my regular Wednesday afternoon visit was, "Can we get going now?"

Before saying hello, she gave instructions. "I need some candy and I want to get ice cream. We need to go now." Despite being a woman of few words, she was insistent and exacting.

Her instructions were given as if the idea of afternoon shopping was a new thought she wanted to implant in my mind, a new idea that I needed to know; something different than the usual routine. In fact, we had been going out each visit for candy and ice cream for the past few months.

Mom grew anxious if there appeared to be any delay in our departure. If I stopped to address a staff member or another resident at the home, she immediately became agitated.

"Let's get going. We don't have much time you know," she told me. This was her time. It was my job to take here out, the sooner the better. I could converse with other people on my own time, not hers.

When I was too slow to respond, she wheeled herself over to the door. As she attempted to leave the premise without me, a bell sounded at the door activated by her wristband. She was prone to attempt to leave without supervision and was wired to the alarm. The safety of wandering residents was a reasonable concern.

She rarely left the nursing home since confined to a wheel chair. She refused to go out on scheduled resident ventures supervised by the staff. I was the only exception. She expected me to take her out at each visit. I suspected she felt less like a nursing home resident and more like a pampered mother when her son took her shopping.

Mom didn't need to go anywhere. She liked to go out. She often complained, when words were available to her, that she felt confined at the home with strangers she didn't like, and "getting out" allowed her to "feel like a regular person".

"Why do I have to live here in this hospital?" she often asked me

"It's not a hospital, it's like a resort," I answered. "You deserve the best now," I reassured her. That seemed to satisfy her until the next visit.

Ice cream at the Dairy Queen and candy at the drug store were our destinations of choice for an afternoon of shopping. Occasionally we changed routines out of necessity when she needed a dress or socks or new underwear. I avoided these ventures unless absolutely necessary. Mostly Mom said she just enjoyed "shopping" with her favorite son.

"I want a cup of vanilla ice cream and no chocolate sauce," she told me for the umpteenth time as we approached the

Dairy Queen restaurant. Her desires never changed. "Then I need some chocolate kisses," she would add.

She used to want her ice cream in a cone but lost the ability to hold the cone. The one time recently we tried a cone, the ice cream ended up in her lap after one energetic lick. She lost her sense of balance. The cup was also difficult. Holding it while eating with a spoon often proved more than she could handle and the ice cream also fell into her lap. She was at her best when the spoon was up-side down.

She ate ice cream in large mouthfuls. She preferred to devour it as quickly as possible. I told her she would get a headache. I don't know for sure where I learned that but I think she once told me.

"I don't know what you are talking about," was her usual reply. She continued with huge mouthfuls until it was gone.

Unless I paid strict attention, Mom had the annoying habit of throwing the empty cup, the napkin, and the spoon out the car window as soon as she was finished eating. I asked her why she did that.

"Do what? She asked.

"Why did you throw the cup out the window?"

"I didn't do that," she insisted. She sounded indignant.

"Yes you did," I reminded her as I opened the door and retrieved the empty cup, spoon, and napkin.

"I don't know what you are talking about," she stated.

No amount of arguing, pleading, or reminding ever changed the situation. I tried to remember to keep the window shut, but if not, out went the empty cup after every visit to Dairy Queen.

Mom particularly enjoyed Hershey chocolate kisses, the small tear drop candy wrapped in tin foil. I never new for sure if these were her favorites or the only ones she could remember by name. No matter.

"I need my candy now," I would be reminded as soon as we left the Dairy Queen parking lot.

"I know. We're going there next," I said.

"I need three bags," she ordered.

Without fail, she always ordered three bags. "I only have enough money for one today," I would tell her.

It was a diversionary tactic. I knew if I had gotten three bags she would have eaten all three by that evening. I didn't give in and I didn't feel guilty. In a few days, during my next visit, we would be back for another bag of kisses. I gave her a handful of candies while we drove back to the home. The front floor boards of the truck were littered with tiny pieces of aluminum foil. The rest of the bag I gave to the staff to dole out intermittently, a few each day.

"Why do we have to go back now?" Mom always asked as we arrived in front of the nursing home.

"Because I have to go back to work," was my reason. She accepted that with little additional resistance. Lifting her out of the truck and into her wheelchair just about exhausted what energy I had remaining. In a few days, we would repeat the routine – arrive at the nursing home, lift her out of the chair and into the truck, drive to Dairy Queen, retrieve the empty cup and napkin, purchase one and not three bags of kisses, make the usual excuses for returning to the home, and lift her out of the truck and back into the wheelchair.

"Why do we have to go home now?" Mom incessantly asked.

Mom never tired of our shopping trips.

* * *

Most people never get an early diagnosis of dementia. They don't have time to prepare for the effects of the disease. Once the diagnosis has been made, they are past the point of making adequate preparations physically, emotionally, or spiritually. They have already entered into that stage where they are protected from its effects, when people have already begun to acknowledge them as a child, a person without resources, someone less than fully human, left out of conversations, left out of social activities, and subject to patronizing attitudes.

The result of this marginalizing of their humanness is that if they don't retreat into silence or depression, then they become confrontational and combative, displaying challenging behavior. Mom displayed both of these tendencies at different times. I never knew which personality would be prevalent on any particular visit.

Managing Mom's Teeth

I noticed immediately that Mom did not have her false teeth in her mouth. She had both upper and lower bridges that she often forgot to wear. Without her teeth, her lips were drooping and sunken. Her mouth was curled inward. She had that floppy mouth look that comes when one's lips have nothing to support them, nothing to lean up against. She looked like Gabby Hayes.

"Hello Peter," she said. Her articulation sounded muted as if she were speaking through a sponge. Without her teeth, Mom appeared so much older than her eighty years. It wasn't just that she looked older, it was that she was unkempt, teeth missing, hair uncombed, and a dress with stains on it.

She took great pride in her false teeth. She kept them exceptionally clean. She had them repaired immediately if they got chipped or broken. They fitted her mouth well and enhanced her smile. People commented on her smile and she knew it was because her teeth were straight, white, and well maintained. She tried her best to keep them that way.

Mom had always had false teeth. When I was a child, I remembered that she kept them in a drinking glass next to her bed each night. I was told she had her real teeth removed because they were crooked. I was fascinated by Mom's teeth. When she was napping and they lay in the glass, I would pick them up, touch the porcelain finish, and attempt to see how the teeth were attached to the plastic-looking gums. I never fully understood how some people's teeth came out and others were permanently attached.

At the nursing home, Mom often forgot her teeth and left them lying around in the most unlikely places. I once found them under her bed covers. She must have slept on them all night. She left them in the bathroom, in other people's rooms, or in the dining hall. One time I found them on the seat of her wheelchair. She had been sitting on them all day. Luckily they did not break. Often they would magically appear under her pillow as if offered to the tooth fairy.

When Mom greeted me she was all gums.

"Mom," I asked her. "What happened to your teeth? Do you know where they are?"

"I don't know what you are talking about," she responded.

"Your teeth," I said. "Your teeth are not in your mouth."

She looked at me for a moment as if attempting to contemplate fully what I was saying. "I lost them." It was recognition that she understood what I was saying as well as acknowledging that she did have teeth, but didn't know at the moment where they were. It was progress.

The search was on. I looked in the bathroom, on the floor under her bed, in her sweater pockets, and in the drawers of her bureau. Nothing. Mom interrupted my search.

"What are you looking for?" she asked.

"Your teeth," I responded.

"I don't know what you are talking about," she said.

I kept looking.

"I really don't need them," Mom stated.

"Of course you do," I told her. Then suddenly I realized that all her food was pureed, mashed to the consistency of baby food, by the nursing home staff. Too many times she had choked on simple foods like carrots, crackers, or string beans. It was a matter of safety to mash her food. Meat was also out of the question unless it was ground up like pudding. She didn't have to chew. She really did not need teeth.

More was at stake than chewing. Her appearance was altered with no teeth. Over the past few months, it was becoming too easy to just ignore the many, small, seemingly non-essential things, like the clothes she wore, the length of her toenails, the cleanliness of the cup that held her teeth at night, the holes in her sweaters, the dribbles of food left on her wheelchair. Individually, these items seemed inconsequential; they didn't matter much. Taken together, however, they were becoming significant. Her personal hygiene was deplorable.

I was feeling that this growing accumulation of small incidents when lumped together comprised a significant deterioration negatively affecting Mom's well being. Her self-respect was affected. One day without her teeth mattered little. A second and third day and perhaps longer soon became the norm rather than the exception. Holes in her clothes, unkempt hair, and stains on bed sheets became acceptable and no longer noticed.

Continued neglect, I feared, would lead to more serious problems like forgetting to take medications, poor diet choices, sleeping all day, and lack of exercise. It is the accumulation of negative experiences which would soon add up to one large overwhelming problem which might be past the time to correct. I needed to pay more attention to the small things. Once she became lax in one area of personal care, it would certainly escalate easily to a lack of complete care.

"Mom," I said. "We have to find your teeth."

"I don't know what you are talking about," she responded.

With no help from her, I found them in the bathroom behind the toilet. I cleaned them and insisted she wear them. Reluctantly she placed them in her mouth.

It continued to be a personal crusade I embarked on with limited results. On most visits, I found Mom without her teeth. I realized that her "care" was not hers alone, that the staff was largely responsible for the lax in hygiene. I notified them of my concern.

* * * *

There is much evidence that the first signs of eventual dementia may be physical rather than mental. If we expect that the early signs of dementia will affect thinking and cognition, we may be surprised. Some of the early warning signs revolve around physical changes rather than mental abilities. Changes in balance, hand grips, and the ability to get out of a chair become clear indicators, and perhaps contributors, to advancing dementia. There remains some controversy about which comes first. Does dementia causes physical challenges or does lack of physical activity lend itself to evolving dementia? They are probably interconnected.

I am convinced that Mom's lack of attention to her physical self contributed to her dementia. Her whole life, she remained inactive and sedentary, more committed to pills than exercise. Diet was lax and addictions to cigarettes and alcohol were prevalent – more than prevalent, they were overwhelming.

Walks with Mom

Mom didn't like to walk. She never liked walking. She said walking was a waste of time and energy. She preferred riding. If she wanted or needed to go someplace, she would rather drive or be driven. If it hinted at exercise, she begged off.

One time in her mid forties she had an epiphany. She decided she needed exercise. She took up ice skating. She told us she used to skate often as a young girl. She bought new skates and went to an ice rink. She only went once. She never returned. We donated the skates to the girl scouts. It was never mentioned in her presence again.

She used to drive herself, but at age sixty five, driving the car became a safety issue. She never admitted to being an unsafe driver.

"Like hell I can't drive," she announced each time we mentioned the safety issue. "I can drive just as good or better than any teenager." We knew differently.

After my father retired, he did all the driving. For him, it was as much a chauvinistic attitude as it was a safety issue. He had little else to do and driving gave him a feeling of control.

Mom got little practice driving. The medications and other drugs she had grown used to taking cut her reaction time. They made her sluggish behind the wheel. Like a person, who after a few drinks, thinks they are invincible, the medications gave Mom a false sense of confidence. She insisted she was an excellent driver. Riding with her became a nightmare.

"Mom, you just went through a stop sign," I told her.

"Like hell I did. There was no stop sign."

You could not win an argument with her.

I visited my parents one time while they still lived in a trailer in North Carolina. My father had a hernia operation and was confined to the hospital for a few days. I stayed with Mom until Pop's expected return.

Mom announced that she needed some things from the grocery store. I volunteered to fetch them.

"No," she insisted. "I can drive myself." There was no future in arguing. "Your father never lets me drive anymore but there is nothing he can do about it now. I'll go myself."

I knew trouble was in the making as I watched her back out of the driveway. I decided to follow her in my rental car. After she turned the first corner, I pulled out of the parking lot and followed her at a distance. It was twilight. She would not recognize my car.

Staying to the right side of the road was a challenge for her. She consistently weaved over the center line and into the opposite lane. She cut in front of oncoming traffic as she made left hand turns. She missed a stop sign. Parallel parking near the grocery store was a disaster. She took up two spaces and left the car standing about five feet from the curb. She managed to return home without incident, but my heart beat wildly as I watched from a distance.

When both parents moved to the Texas retirement village, we refused to allow her to drive. She protested vehemently, but soon acquiesced. She never asked again.

Not only did she give up driving, she gave up walking as well. It was as if she had suddenly and thoroughly been struck with an "immobility syndrome." She avoided walking whenever she could. When she did walk – to the dining room, to the bathroom, toward an ashtray, she claimed it was a "chore". Her days were spent lying on the sofa while reading or watching television or sleeping. She complained that walking gave her cramps or other intestinal disorders. Her doctor could find no symptoms of anything wrong. He suggested she try walking to relieve the stomach discomfort.

"He doesn't know what he is talking about," she exclaimed. "I'm too sick to walk."

"Maybe you feel sick because you don't get any exercise," we attempted to insert into her thinking.

"Walking only makes me feel worse," she replied. "Besides, if walking is such a great thing, why did God invent the wheel?"

It was never determined why she wouldn't or couldn't walk, she just didn't. It wasn't long before she refused to walk even when necessary. She chose a wheelchair. She convinced other people to push her; no she demanded they push her. When she had to stand up, she needed help. If left alone while standing, her legs buckled under her. I had to lift her physically under the arms and move her from the wheelchair into the front seat of my car each time we left the nursing home. I kept encouraging her.

"Try to walk a little, Mom," I would suggest as I helped her up. "Just move the legs a little."

"I can't," she insisted. "I don't know what you are talking about."

Eventually I gave up and stopped asking. I assumed she would continue to resist and insist she couldn't walk.

Pushing Mom in her wheelchair throughout the nursing home soon became old for other residents. Staff members showed her how to propel herself by using her arms and hands to push the large wheels.

"That's right. Use your arms to push the wheels foreword and then lift your arms backward and do it again," they told her. They demonstrated the process.

"I can't do that," she insisted. Her resistance was adamant. She pleaded with staff and passing residents to help her get where she wanted to go. Sometimes they refused and Mom swore at them and stayed immobile.

Mom eventually gave in. One day I saw her in the hallway using the hand rails to propel herself in her wheelchair. She grabbed the rail and pulled the chair about four feet. She then repeated the process until she noticed me watching her.

"Mom," I said. You're moving on your own."

Embarrassed to be caught, she replied, "I don't know what you are talking about."

Mom made steady progress. She soon learned to use her legs while sitting in the chair to "walk" the chair forward. She had enough friction on the souls of her slippers and enough power in her legs to move slowly foreword in a kind of walking gesture while she remained sitting in the chair. I did not comment on her progress feeling that any recognition would discourage her. She had an image to maintain. If it wasn't her idea solely, she would quit trying.

Mom practiced walking in her chair each day until she became quite proficient. I suspect her greatest motivation was a lack of response from other residents and staff to her inquiries about pushing her. They continued to refuse. But she was determined to get to the smoking parlor. That was motivation enough.

Occasionally, I relinquished and pushed Mom around a pathway outside. It covered much of the grounds, was shaded by live oak trees, and in the spring Bluebonnets were in bloom. The path ended down a slight, but long, incline.

On this day, I was holding onto Mom's wheelchair preventing it from going down the incline to quickly. Bicycle type rubber grips were on each hand hold. I was holding the grips. Suddenly both grips slipped off the metal handles and I was left holding only the grips. I watched in horror as Mom's chair – with Mom in it – began rolling swiftly down the incline. Her speed increased with each section of the walk way.

I ran frantically after her but was not able to catch up to her until her chair rolled off the walkway and the front wheels were buried in the soft grass. Mom pitched forward onto her stomach.

Before I could reach down to help her, I noticed Mom was moving her legs. She propped them under her body in an effort to gain balance and then tried to stand up. It was a deliberate movement. She almost made it. When she noticed me reaching to help her, she collapsed and sat back on the grass. There she remained until I picked her up.

Mom appeared no worse for the wear, maybe a few grass stains, but no broken bones or bruises that I could see.

"Damn it Peter. Why don't you watch what you are doing?" She immediately scolded me.

What surprised me was how quickly she reacted from the fall. Almost immediately her legs were functional. In the moment of crisis her agility returned. After years of refusing to walk and at least one year in a wheelchair, suddenly there was activity in her extremities. I felt as if I were not there she would have gotten herself up and perhaps walked home.

"Let's go back so I can have a cigarette," Mom said. I placed her in the wheelchair and she insisted I push her toward the front door.

Thanksgiving Diner

I didn't want Mom to be alone on a holiday. The nursing home celebrated holidays with decorations and special meals, but since Pop had died there was no family connection there for Mom. Holidays were meant to be spent with family. I was intent on keeping that tradition alive, partly for Mom's sake but also to appease my own sense of guilt. It was my decision that put Mom in the nursing home and I never fully accepted that decision

Mom had no expectations about holidays. Most times she had no idea what day it was much less that the day might be a holiday. Reminding her it was Thanksgiving made no impression.

It was a risky venture to take Mom outside the nursing home. She no longer walked. I had to transport a wheelchair. She had difficulty sitting upright in the car and she was incontinent. These presented severe obstacles whenever I took Mom outside the home.

But Thanksgiving would not seem complete without Mom's presence, without grandma as part of the celebration. So we took Thanksgiving to Mom. My wife, my two daughters, a friend, and I went to the nursing home for a Thanksgiving dinner.

Mom ate most of her food pureed. Since she refused to chew, it was necessary to mash her food into one thick soup. This day – Thanksgiving – was all about turkey. I wanted Mom to try some "real food" - turkey meat that looked like turkey meat. I asked the staff for other "real foods" I thought Mom could eat – cranberry sauce, mashed potatoes, cooked string beans, and pumpkin pie for desert. We ate in the main dining room. It was decorated in festive fall colors. Paper leaves covered the table and a small folded crape paper turkey was a centerpiece.

The staff reminded me of Mom's dietary expectations. I needed to be careful what she ate. I assured them I would take all precautions. I would watch her carefully.

With great anticipation we awaited Thanksgiving dinner with Mom and the rest of my family. Bring on the food. Bring on the good times.

The turkey looked scrumptious. It was covered in gravy. I put Mom's bib on and she immediately began shoveling large hunks of turkey meat into her mouth. Fortunately she had her false teeth in her mouth.

"Go slowly, Mom," I urged her. "You don't want to choke."

"Leave me alone," she responded. "I don't know what you are talking about."

Despite my pleading for her to take small bites and chew thoroughly, she continued to devour turkey meat and peas and cranberry sauce in great quantities.

Suddenly she sat bolt upright in her chair. Her face turned a red hue and her lips became blue. She was chocking and gasping for air.

"Mom," I yelled. "Mom, are you alright?"

My first thoughts were that she would quickly swallow what was caught in her throat and all would be well again. That's what I hoped That didn't happen and she continued changing colors and gasping for air. She had a frightened stare in her eyes.

I panicked and yelled for a nurse. My wife tried unsuccessfully to get her to spit up but she was uncooperative. Two staff people came rushing to our table. A large male attendant picked Mom up from her chair, turned her away from him, and started the Heimlich maneuver. Mom struggled a few seconds more trying to breathe. Her face showed the agony of being crushed by the maneuver of the attendant. Suddenly, with a volcanic thrust, out popped a large hunk of half devoured turkey meat and sailed across the table. It landed in my lap. Mom started breathing again and a normal color returned to her face and lips. She smiled. Her teeth stayed in her mouth.

We all sat very still for a few minutes. Despite my lack of action, I felt exhausted. We looked at each other in a way that communicated, "thank God she's alright." We were beginning to comprehend what happened. By this time, Mom's breathing was again normal although she continued to cough sporadically and emit gurgling sounds.

We relaxed. "That was a close call," my daughter remarked.

"Wow. We almost lost grandma," the other daughter chimed in.

It was then I noticed Mom holding her fork with another large piece of turkey stuck to it and she immediately shoved it into her mouth. All four of us reached toward her and my wife stuck her fingers in Mom's mouth and pulled out the piece of turkey meat.

"Why did you do that?" Mom said indignantly. "This is Thanksgiving and I want some more turkey."

I realized that Mom had not forgotten about Thanksgiving. She did, however, forget how to chew. Each time thereafter we celebrated a holiday with Mom, we did so with more discretion and with pureed food.

6

Like a Practical Joke Gone Horribly Wrong

"My memory's not as sharp as it used to be. Also, my memory's not as sharp as it used to be." ...Author unknown

"It seems strange, and I guess that it sounds quite neurotic, That I'm plagued with emotions, so often chaotic, That all I'm aware of are feelings that swell, And I'm often not sure of the story they tell." ...Author Unknown

Society does not accord much esteem for the elderly. Rather than being revered they become a burden. If aging itself is a burden, imagine our response to the elderly crippled with dementia. It's double jeopardy.

People with dementia are riddled with stigmas. Foremost among them is the loss of power. Those in our society without power are accorded the lowest status. Dementia robs the person of power and renders that person weak, inflexible, and unproductive. In society, that's being at the bottom of the rung.

Dementia sucks. Like a practical joke gone horribly wrong, dementia robs a person of all dignity and self-respect rendering the person defenseless and vulnerable and beset by continual frustration. We don't have compassion, we have pity. Society views them as powerless, people whose existence is barely beyond vegetative.

Because communication is garbled and confused, their behaviors are often bizarre. They become objects of distortion. It's fun to mimic them, to laugh at their strange behavior as if they were clowns.

"Doctor Ryan tells his patient, Muriel, 'Well I have good news and bad news.'
Muriel responds, 'Tell me Doc. What's the bad news?'
You have Alzheimer's disease.'
'Good heavens!' exclaims Muriel, ' So, what's the good news?'
'You can go home and forget about it.' says Dr Ryan."
…Author Unknown

The loss of memory leads to a loss of the past. Those with dementia have difficulty recalling their history or telling their stories. People no longer talk *with* them; they talk *to them* as if they were objects and not persons. We think of those with dementia as totally immune to ridicule, as devoid of humanness, and as merely inanimate objects. We fear these people because they often reflect a side of ourselves we don't want to recognize.

Debbie Everett, A Canadian hospital chaplain has understood this well:

"People with dementia are magic mirrors where I have seen my human condition and have repudiated the commonly held societal values of power and prestige that are unreal and shallow…because people with dementia have their egos stripped from them; their unconscious comes very close to the surface. They, in turn, show us the masks behind which we hide our authentic personhood from the world."
…Everett, Deborah, *Forget me not: the spiritual care of people with Alzheimer's,* Inkwell Press, Edmonton, 1996, p. 167)

Mom developed dementia big time. It didn't occur all at once, but over time her ability to communicate, to complete sentences, make decisions, recognize people, react to experiences, and recall her past diminished severely. Dementia captured her life and rendered her incapable to controlling her own destiny. Clearly, as the dementia developed, her social status and personal identity took a nose dive. The people she knew, myself included, had difficulty relating to her as a mature adult rather than as a child. She relinquished her independence and became fully reliant on the whims of others. All sense of power she might have held; the power to make her own decisions, the power over her own body – the power to control such simple matters as when to get up, what to wear, what to eat, and when to go to bed – she surrendered to someone else.

Dementia had the effect of an interloper in Mom's life. Like a trespasser, it encroached upon her mind to steal from it all avenues of growth. It specifically invaded the memory, but the consequences affected the whole person. She lost her ability for conversation, a key element in socialization. Her relationships began to disintegrate. The loss of memory frustrated her desire for sharing in family experiences and traditions, and all but eliminated emotional ties to friends. It demanded complete dependency on outside assistance while at the same time caused her to thwart attempts by those who wished to help.

Her dementia was a great challenge for me. I had to recognize and accept Mom's dementia as the uninvited guest that it was. Never an easy task for me. She was never a cooperative person, but the dementia made matters even worse. She either ignored or resisted most attempts I made for improvement in her health and happiness. I was a "fixer" by nature and dementia was not a fixable experience. I lived continuously those last years with the hope that life for Mom would be a contented, peaceful, and joyful experience. Other than the fact that she was so totally unaware of what was going on around her, life was anything but pleasant.

Mom's dementia also challenged my tendency to allow it to dehumanize her in my estimation or in the perception of others. I felt a great empathy for staff members at the nursing home who were subjected to her bizarre behavior. I continued to feel conflicted between accepting their demeaning care as the best they could do under the circumstances while not allowing for patronizing attitudes toward her despite her sickness. There was little I could do to treat her disease, but much that I could resist as a consequence of its symptoms.

I often observed family members of other patients who suffered with some degree of dementia. It appeared they thought it futile to try to rationalize with the person. Conversations were one way and limited. The family talked about their mother but not to their mother; it was as if she were not present. Derogatory terms slipped into their speech, perhaps unintentionally. These bungling attempts at conversation excluded their mother and often belittled and ridiculed her, sometimes making her the butt of jokes.

"Mother has lost her mind and we don't know where to look for it." Or "She doesn't understand what's going on. She lives in another world."

I was not always able to rise above the attitude of patronizing Mom; my patience was tried and found wanting many times. Despite my meager attempts at sensitivity, I still managed to fall captive to the lure of dementia. Her behavior raised feelings of frustration and irritability that I often found uncontrollable. Many experiences were simply embarrassing both for her and for me. Her loss of memory and inability to recall her history caused me to wonder if any thoughts occurred to her at all. I was surprised by the outcome. Perhaps most distressing was not her loss of memory or recognition, but rather how I responded to her. Upon deep reflection, I often wished for a "do over".

Going Home

Memory can be selective. We all remember some things better than we remember others. Sometimes, I surprise myself when memories come rushing back that I thought I had long ago forgotten.

When dementia sets in, memory all but fades away completely. So I thought but Mom recalled at least one memory that resuscitated itself. For her, it was bitter sweet. For me it played on my guilt feelings until I felt overwhelmed.

Mom had been living at the nursing facility nine years. Only occasionally did she recall living anywhere else and then only when pestered by my incessant questions.

"Mom, do you remember the house at Water Island?" I wanted to check the status of her memory. For twenty years, every summer was spent at a cottage my parents owned on a small barrier island off the South coast of Long Island. Mom loved it there. She grew up nearby and held fond memories of the place and people. She asked that her ashes be spread there upon her demise, a promise I never kept.

"Do you remember Water Island?" I asked again.

"Of course I do," she responded. "What about it?"

To challenge her memory further, I asked, "What about the house in Cedar Grove? Do you remember that house?"

Cedar Grove was the town where she lived permanently for over forty-five years. It was where I grew up along with my two brothers and where she had most of her friendships. When I asked again, "What do you remember about the house in Cedar Grove?" she had a puzzled look on her face.

"Nothing," she replied. "What's a Cedar Grove?"

Mom's memory had grown very selective and inconsistent. She never instigated recollections about anything. It was as if her memory slate had been wiped clean. Once in a great while, she could respond to a suggestion that triggered a reflection or a remembrance, but without reciting details.

I had another theory for her memory loss. Despite knowing of her dementia and its associated loss of memory, I still thought that perhaps memories were repressed because they were painful. Even good memories can be distressing when one realizes they are in the past never to be relived again. I intentionally avoided any discussion of experiences in her life I knew were unpleasant. Still Mom appeared vacant, unable or unwilling to reminisce. Any hope I maintained that fond recollections might serve to bring some peace and contentment and joy into her aging life were not to be realized.

During these past nine years, her primary connection with her past was my father's presence. She would sit by his side each day in the nursing home parlor while he read the National Geographic Magazine or his daily newspaper. They hardly talked except for Mom's incessant pestering of him for a cigarette. I didn't know if she really knew who he was other than that he looked familiar and offered consistency in her daily life and she felt comfortable in his presence.

After Pop died, I thought she would miss him terribly. She didn't. I prompted her with questions about him to test her memory.

"Mom, do you miss Pop," I asked

"Who?" she replied.

I never got an affirmative answer. She said she didn't know who I was talking about. The dementia sapped her memory of her husband of sixty- five years. I felt very sad.

On this particular day, Mom seemed very anxious. She couldn't sit still in her chair. She insisted on rolling as close to my seat as she could get, right up against my shins. Each time I pushed her back, she returned to that position again until my shins began to ache. She kept this up until I had to place a small table between us to protect my legs from further damage. I recognized that something was bothering her as she did not act like this during our previous visits the past two weeks.

"Peter." She said. I was surprised that she called me by name; an indication of clear recognition. "Peter, I want to go home. Can you take me to your home today?"

This caught me off guard. I was thoroughly surprised. At no time during the past year, since the death of my father, had Mom ever mentioned going to my home. It would have surprised me if she even knew I had a home somewhere nearby. My appearances at the nursing home for visits with her seemed almost magical judging from the state of her dementia. I just appeared. I had hesitated taking her to my house for fear that it might upset her familiar routine. Routine seemed to keep her clam and satisfied. She enjoyed our outings for ice cream and candy, but never requested to come to my house.

"Why do you want to come to my house?" I asked innocently. I then added, "I don't think that would be a good idea."

"Why can't I go?" she asked. Then she added a stinger. "I can't stand to live in this rat hole even for another day. Please, if you love me, please take me home with you."

Mom was relentless. She pleaded. She begged. "Please, I have to go live at your house. I can't stand it here any longer."

No matter the excuses I offered – "I don't have room at my housed. There is no one home during the day to take care of what you need. I don't have a bathroom you can use easily" – she persisted. I asked her why she wanted to live at my house, but got no reasoned response.

"If you really loved me, you would take me home right now," she kept saying over and over.

My first thoughts were that something had happened that frightened her terribly. Perhaps in a moment of mental clarity she recalled Pop's death. Perhaps she had an epiphany of sorts and suddenly remembered she had a family. I could only imagine what went through her mind that triggered this outburst. Conceivably she thought that moving to my home was the only remedy to alleviate her fears. I wasn't sure. I could only speculate.

"Has something frightened you?" I asked her.

"No. I don't know what you are talking about," she replied. She continued with her pleading. "Please take me home with you right now."

I could decipher no reason for her request, but her persistence was unremitting and unnerving. I needed to know why she suddenly had this uncontrollable compulsion, this myopic focus on living at my house.

Mom could not live at my house. It was a bad idea. In fact, it might even be cruel. My wife and I worked days. Mom would be alone with no one to feed her, change her Depends, or assist if she fell down. She couldn't walk by herself, not even to the bathroom. The thought of her sitting all day in a wet or soiled diaper greatly dismayed me. Using a phone was beyond her abilities. We had no funds for hiring a sitter service. The selfish thought also occurred that she would be a considerable disruption in our lives. My wife and I needed alone time together to maintain a stable relationship.

I felt conflicted. If I gave into my mounting guilt and moved Mom in to my home as she requested, I ran the risk of instability in my own family relationships. I could easily imagine the resentment it might cause my wife and children. If I ignored her requests, at least at this moment, I knew I would have difficulty minimizing my guilt. I decided I could live with the guilt. Mom would have to stay at the nursing facility.

"Please, please take me home," Mom continued to plead.

My mind was made up, she was staying put. To appease her momentarily, I promised her I would talk with my wife to see what we could do. I was balking. It was a diversionary tactic, a stalling technique. I needed some time to figure out what might be bothering her; what was fueling her desire and sudden urge to want to live with us. Why, after so long a period of complete doldrums, did Mom suddenly become fixated on leaving the nursing home?

Her pleadings had turned to tears. She was visibly upset and disappointed that I balked at her immediate request. She wasn't asking for the unreasonable – a trip to Disneyland, to buy her a new house of her own, or to abandon my wife. But what she was asking I knew would radically change my life. My promise to talk about it further didn't appease Mom, so she abruptly turned her wheelchair around and began propelling herself down the hall and back toward her room.

I left the home feeling confused. No good son would deny his mother's pleading to take care of her in her old age. She should be living at her son's home. Rationally I knew otherwise. Living at my home was not in her best interests. What to do?

After a sleepless night, I called the nursing home social worker. Lynn impressed me as having good insight. I related to her my conversations with Mom and my conflicted attitudes.

"Would you be willing to speak with my mother? See if you can tell if she is serious or if this is just some passing illusion," I asked her.

I wanted her to probe, as best as she was able, and try to determine if Mom was aware of my father's death. Was her anxiousness and request in response to this sudden awareness?

"Sure," she said. "Let me have a chat with her and I'll get back to you."

Anxious to know what Lynn had learned, I called her the next morning.

"Yes, I had time to talk with her yesterday afternoon. She made no mention of wanting to move. I tried giving hints to encourage her to talk about how she felt about leaving here and living with you, but she only said 'I don't know what you are talking about.' I don't think there is anything to be concerned about. She made no mention of your dad."

I thanked Lynn.

I visited with Mom regularly after this experience and never, not even when prompted by me with questions about living at the nursing home, did Mom mention she wanted to leave the facility. I can only surmise that on that particular day, some connections occurred in her clouded mind that conjured a series of memories; thoughts combined in such a fashion as to trigger strong feelings of desperation. To want to "go home" is a strong emotion, for most people. Mom is still a person despite the dementia.

* * * *

Dementia causes considerable distress. In addition to a depletion of one's mental capacity, it also greatly diminishes physical abilities. I can only imagine how much becoming incontinent can be embarrassing and demeaning. Despite that we may *think* that it doesn't matter to the person with dementia, we don't know for sure.

If one's spiritual health is dependent upon feelings of respect, importance, and acceptance imagine how the embarrassment of having your diaper changed as an adult by someone you hardly know can affect your attitude and feelings of self-worth. Mom suffered from dementia. She also suffered from incontinence. I wondered what effect dementia played in her spiritual journey.

Shopping For Dresses

"Peter, I have to get some new dresses," Mom announced as I walked into her room for my regular Wednesday visit. She said this as if it was a long held desire she had been reflecting on but mentally repressed for a long time. "I don't have anything to wear," she continued. She reminded me of my own daughters when they worried about having an outfit for the senior prom.

Regardless of when I might visit, Mom always assumed I was there to take her shopping. Most times she merely expected to go our for ice cream at the local Dairy Queen followed by a few chocolate kisses from the bag I bought at the pharmacy. Clothes shopping with Mom was a bit more challenging. Socks, underwear, pull-over tops and everyday wear that didn't need to be tried on or fitted exactly, these I could manage with little complications. Dresses required more acumen, more expertise, and some physical gymnastics.

"Okay Mom, we'll go shopping for a dress," I acquiesced. I knew she would continue to insist relentlessly until I gave in. I resigned myself that I would get it over as soon as possible. Today was the day.

Mom's incontinence put a wrinkle in how long we could be absent from the nursing facility. I needed staff assistance when she needed to be changed. Changing my mother's diaper was beyond my pay scale. Before leaving the home, I always asked a staff aide if she had changed Mom's Depends – an adult diaper. She also wore a pair of tight panties over the diaper, a precaution taken to keep the diaper from falling down.

Mom protested when I asked a staff aide to check to see that she was "dressed appropriately" for going outside. I sensed she knew that meant a diaper check and that must have brought on some embarrassment no matter how often it occurred. Once she was dressed, she rarely complained about the diapers. The arrangement worked well and allowed for considerable mobility once we left the nursing home.

The department store, Weiner's, was only a few miles away. Weiner's specialized in "simple" clothes for mature women. They had a nice assortment of larger sizes and easy-on clothes. Clothing without buttons or zippers worked best for Mom. Their inexpensive prices added to their appeal. It was her favorite store. She liked shopping there because she could reach the clothing racks. Mom recognized where we were headed.

Today, however, she seemed a bit sullen. In the car, she shifted her body frequently as if sitting on something uncomfortable. I asked, "Mom, you alright? Is something bothering you?"

"I'm fine," she responded sounding a bit agitated. "Let's get to the store."

Because I was her official driver, I was able to secure a parking spot in the handicap zone close to the store entrance. I brought her wheelchair but she refused to use it. It was with great difficulty I got her out of the car and began the short walk to the doorway. I had to hold her every step of the way. Along the way, she constantly stopped momentarily before moving on. There was a grimace on her face.

"You sure you want to do this?" I asked. "You look upset about something. Why do you keep stopping?"

"I'm fine. Let's go shopping," she insisted.

We approached the front door. A young woman held the door open for us.

"Welcome to Weiners," she said as Mom and I walked past her and into the store

It was unusually busy with shoppers. There was a dress sale happening. Just as we reached the first row of dresses, a strange look came over Mom's face as if she suddenly remembered that she forgot something. She began struggling with her clothes, pulling at the waist of her dress with both hands.

"What's the matter, Mom? I asked. She didn't respond. She stood absolutely still.

At that very moment I looked down at Mom's feet. Hanging at the bottom of Mom's legs, as if about to trip her if she took even the slightest step forward, was her Depends. I could see it was "loaded." I could smell it. A flash of great embarrassment suddenly overtook me and, for a moment, I wasn't sure what to do. I wanted to run and hide behind a rack of clothes that stood nearby, pretend I was not with Mom, and look innocent as if picking out a coat for myself.

I didn't run. I knew I could not leave Mom alone. My personal embarrasment turned quickly into empathy. How humiliated Mom must feel. I reached down, grabbed the wet and brown stained diaper and pulled it gently from around her shoes.

"What are you doing down there?" Mom sounded indignant. I suddenly realized she was unaware of her dilemma.

"Just checking on something," I told her. "Hold still for a minute"

I tried not to yank on the diaper for fear of knocking Mom down. I pulled the diaper free from her shoes. I picked it up but it dripped leaving a yellow pool on the floor. I folded it in half hoping nothing solid would fall on the floor. I stuffed the whole thing in my jacket pocket. A dozen persons pretended not to watch what was happening.

"Mom, we have to leave," I said. I grabbed Mom's arms and attempted to escort her toward the door. She resisted.

"Why are we leaving?" she asked.

"We have to go back to the car right now," I insisted without explanation.

"We came all this way to buy me a new dress and now you're taking me back to the car. What about my dress?" Mom was clearly disappointed.

I didn't have the heart to explain the details of what happen. She wouldn't have believed me anyway.

* * * *

I might have assumed that Mom had no awareness of the situation she just experienced. Her dementia got in the way. If she was unaware, then she must not have been adversely affected or greatly embarrassed. But do we know for sure? I did not know to what degree she was affected by the experience because her dementia prevented her from expressing her feelings. Can we assume that the embarrassment held no bearing on her feelings of dignity? Better yet, can I assume that she did feel embarrassment but could not articulate it?

Spirituality gives form to dignity. A person's sense of worth stems from their level of spirituality. Because Mom lost her ability to articulate her feelings is no reason to assume that she did not feel the loss of dignity from the shopping experience. She very well might have regained some dignity by continuing to shop for a dress she so much desired, but my own embarrassment and loss of dignity prevented that from happening. Sometimes when dealing with those suffering from dementia, we allow our own feelings to take precedence over the other. Yes, the behavior of someone with dementia can be exasperating and dysfunctional, but we must remember that person retains a humanness that emanates from their spirituality.

One of the great gifts of spirituality is its ability to cause you to look inward. I discovered resources internally I never knew existed. Even if I considered myself to be small and insignificant, I discovered that I was greater than I ever imagined; more powerful, more significant, more secure. Mom's spirituality was never tested. I assumed that her dementia rendered her limited and insignificant. She never challenged that assumption.

The Visit

The memory can be a tricky thing. Just when you think you have it mastered, it bites you in the ass. When dementia sets in, the trickery of the memory becomes all the more haphazard. It fails you more often than it serves you.

Whenever I planned a visit with Mom at the nursing home, I would call ahead to notify the staff. I wanted them to have her prepared – up and dressed, hair combed, teeth in her mouth, and a fresh Depends in place in case we were to leave the home for a while. Mom's incontinence was getting worse. The staff obliged me willingly and I appreciated their efforts.

I called the floor staff at the nursing home. "I'll be up for a visit with Roberta, "I told them. "Could you have her clean and ready?"

"Not to worry. We'll have her looking real pretty," they told me. The aide added, "And I'm sure she's looking forward to seeing you."

Mom always had a big, toothy grin whenever she first saw me upon my arrival. I was not sure she remembered when I came or how often, but I was glad she still recognized me.

When I arrived, Mom was not at her usual place in the front room. She often sat in her wheelchair near the doorway leading outside as if waiting for a chance to escape. The door could only be opened by a button too high for her to reach. In addition, she now had a new alarm attached to the back of her wheelchair which sounded if she passed by the "eye" on the door sill. Mom was considered a "safety threat" by the staff, despite that she was confined to a wheelchair, weighed barely a hundred pounds, and often could not remember her own name.

"Where is Mom?" I asked the front room receptionist. All the staff knew Mom.

"I guess they haven't brought her up front yet," She responded.

I started to walk towards the hall leading to Mom's wing. Half way down I could see her wheeling herself, motoring along using her feet to propel her wheelchair. I couldn't help thinking "What kind of threat can she be?"

When she spotted me, she smiled broadly. Both sets of teeth were in her mouth. She had a dress on instead of the bathrobe she liked wearing. She appeared excited.

Mom didn't talk much anymore, but today she was animated. She immediately began telling me about her day.

"What a commotion," she exclaimed. "The nurses were all in a dither. They dressed me in this red dress and brushed my hair. They said Peter liked me in this red dress. They told me Peter was coming and wanted me to look really good." I was confused by her third person speech

"Well, they have done a good job. You do look really nice," I told her. We continued together towards the front room.

We reached the parlor and found a place to sit and park her wheelchair, Mom's excitement continued. "They make such a fuss when they know Peter is coming. Such a commotion. They get me all gussied up because they know I like it when Peter visits." Still she addressed me in the third person.

Such articulation and animation. I hadn't heard so many words from her mouth in months. Lately she had seemed depressed. But that was only my guess because it was difficult to gage what she was feeling. The dementia usually robed her of complete sentences, rendering her often speechless and seemingly emotionless. Today she seemed jovial beyond my imagination and very aware of my visit. I felt like I had a reputation to uphold. I had better make our visit pleasant and memorable.

Suddenly Mom stopped talking. She stared at me, looking very confused. It was as if she noticed something new or strange or that she wasn't aware of about me before this day, a new discovery she was about to disclose to me. Perhaps, I thought, she just remembered something she wanted to tell me. I was hoping her memory would return. In anticipation, I encouraged her to tell me what was on her mind.

"When is Peter coming?" she asked.

* * * *

The spirituality of a person is not eroded by the onset of dementia. The "spirit" remains alive despite that it appears dormant and unresponsive. Spirituality is not exclusive to a religious perspective. It is not one dimension of life but rather permeates and gives meaning to the whole of life. Spirituality is like a frame of reference that keeps all conditions of the person in perspective and provides the power to overcome anxieties, fears, loss, and seemingly unsolvable problems. Spirituality resuscitates the soul of the person.

I wanted to recognize the spirituality still within Mom, to respect her as a unique and whole person. I could not assume that just because the personality changed, the behavior bizarre, and the memory failed, that the core of Mom is diminished of spirituality.

For the person with dementia, it is essential that spirituality become the well from which one must draw whenever one needs to handle the loss events in life. Mom's life was one potential loss after another. She lost her husband as well as any remembrance of him. Incontinence rendered her at a loss of bodily control. Opinions, perspectives, arguments, attitudes, all seemed to disappear.

Dementia does not reduce a person's desire for spirituality, but it does make it difficult to express. Those with dementia have not lost their longing for wholeness and significance in life, but they find it much harder to share these concerns with others. My ability to engage Mom "spiritually" was being severely tested under circumstances I failed to grasp clearly.

The Teddy Bear

A very wise person told me that when people begin to border on dementia, they sometimes find relating to inanimate objects as worthy substitutes for people. Comfort comes with cuddling a teddy bear. That didn't come as a complete surprise. When I walked the halls of the home I had seen many residents sitting alone and mumbling incoherently to themselves while gently stroking a stuffed animal. At first, the idea repulsed me. Such childlike behavior from adults. I wasn't yet convinced that dementia was a permanent mental illness, only a temporary side effect of aging.

I never asked why they held the teddy bear. I thought that demeaning, patronizing, or simply rude. Did I think they were childish, immature, or worse, crazy? Better I ignore questioning and assume that Mrs. Spofford and Mrs. Richie were minding the stuffed animals for their grandchildren.

When I was told that feeble-minded people deeply enmeshed in their dotage relate well to stuffed animals, I didn't think they meant "relate" in the usual sense of the word. I reasoned that the stuffed animal simply provided some relief from constant loneliness.

Mom had isolated herself almost completely. She spent most days alone in her room. That couldn't be good. So... maybe an inanimate companion might sooth her, give her company, create a relationship of some kind. Teddy bears don't have expectations. They don't interrupt. They don't offer helpful opinions that create annoyance. Their feelings are not easily damaged, and they don't take umbrage at rude remarks. The perfect companion. Perhaps pervasive loneliness was Mom's stumbling block to experiencing her spirituality.

"What's that for?" she asked as I placed the fuzzy brown bear with button eyes and a yellow ribbon around its neck on her lap.

"I just thought you might like to have it around. You know, to keep you company. You don't ever have to feel alone if you have this teddy bear"

She immediately threw it on to the bed.

"Why would I want a stuffed animal?" she protested. "That's for children. Do you think I'm a child?"

A glimmer of the old Mom appeared along with some reassurance that there was life in that silent soul. I actually felt good being scolded.

I said no more and left the teddy bear lying on her bed.

I never saw the teddy bear again. When I asked her what happened to it, she would only reply, "I don't know what you are talking about."

Three weeks later Mom greeted me enthusiastically in the front parlor when I arrived for my regular Sunday afternoon visit. She was very excited.

"I want you to meet my new friends," she told me

"Sure," I responded. I had no idea what she meant. She caught me by surprise. "What new friends?" I asked.

"My new friends. They're down the hall. Push me down the hall, and I will show you."

I was curious, but hesitant. Were there truly new friends or was this some imaginary venture conditioned by her dementia.

"Come on," she insisted. I was glad she was animated and articulate today

We set off down the hall toward the day room in her residential wing. We wheeled into the room, and Mom pointed to a large bird cage situated on a high table near the bay window. It was huge, large enough, I thought, to hold a family of monkeys. As we approached the cage, I saw two green parrots perched inside. One was plucking its wing feathers, grooming itself, while the other chewed on a round object I could not identify. Neither paid us much attention.

"That one with the orange beak is Martha," Mom said. "The other one is Ferdinand. I really like them a lot. They're so funny the way they climb around and friendly too."

The cage door was open. Mom stretched her arm toward Ferdinand. The bird hopped on it. She pointed toward Martha again to be sure I saw her.

"These are my new friends, and I'm gonna take good care of them," she told me.

Over the next few months, the staff at the home remarked often about how animated Mom had become since befriending Martha and Ferdinand. She often confused the two bird's names, but no matter. She greeted them each day and introduced them to whoever happened to pass by whether they paid any attention to Mom or not. She talked to the birds and said they talked back to her. Who am I to say otherwise? The two birds were included in any and all conversations I had with Mom as if they were family.

I want to believe that Martha and Ferdinand exorcized the "demons" from Mom, but I am not ready to make that claim. What is of significance is that Martha and Ferdinand provided a connection, a handle that enabled Mom to benefit from the fruits of spirituality even though she was not intentionally seeking it. As one person remarked, "When people of great spirituality meet situations of great challenge, the abstractions of spirituality become the concreteness of coping strategies." The spiritual component of a personality is the function that integrates all other aspects of personhood. Ferdinand and Martha enabled Mom to once again connect to her own spirituality, a task I was never able to achieve without the help of two birds.

Parallel Play

A failing memory plays havoc with family relationships. Mom often forgot who I was despite visiting together regularly. She could not remember where she was living.

"Mom, do you like living here? I would ask. "Do you know where you are living?"

"In Cedar Grove. I live in Cedar Grove. Why are you asking me this?" she would reply.

Mom left Cedar Grove fifteen years ago. When I mentioned the town, she had no recollection.

When Mom recognized me, it was a cursory recollection. She knew the face, but often forgot the name.

"Do you remember who I am, Mom?" I asked her

"Of course I do," she responded immediately. There was silence for a while as she examined my face momentarily then looked away. I could tell she knew me, but struggled with the details.

When Mom mingled with other people, I noticed some very peculiar behaviors. Despite living among other residents and staff who were always present, her behavior seemed more like a person living alone. She acted like a stranger in a crowd. Mom didn't speak to the other residents. Instead she bumped into them. She seemed oblivious of their presence as she motored along in her wheelchair. If she was headed in some direction along the hallways she paid no attention to who might be in front of her until she ran into someone. Without acknowledging responsibility – "Sorry, I didn't see you" – she sought a way around them. What conversation she initiated was limited to "look where you're going" or "what did you do that for?" Other people were objects in the way.

Mom was assigned a special dining area for her meals. Because of her dementia she had to sit at a supervised table that was half rounded so the attendant could sit facing the half dozen residents and assist them while eating. Assistance often meant keeping them from taking food from each other's plates or being available if someone began choking. Despite that her food was pureed, in her haste to eat, Mom often choked.

She sat in the front parlor when she watched television. This was an unsupervised area. She wheeled her chair directly in front of the large screen television, blocking the view of other residents. She became quite upset when a staff member or I would move her out of the way of others.

"Don't do that," she would exclaim. If I were present, I would explain to her that she was blocking the view of other people. It didn't register.

"To hell with them," was her indignant reply.

Reluctantly she attended exercise classes, slide presentations of people's travels, visiting children's choirs, and Sunday chapel. Once placed in position by a staff member, she soon tried to escape from the room. When confronted, re-positioned, and asked why she wanted to leave, she responded, "I don't know what you are talking about."

I could not help but think how closely her behaviors mimicked the child's parallel play experience. Children, at a very young age, when in the presence of other children, do not interact well. They exist side by side, but not interrelated. They exist to each other but not in concert with each other. In a similar way, in the presence of other people, Mom's dementia did not allow her to mutually interact. I don't know if she sought out company, but in their presence, she existed in parallel, not in relationship.

Mom's Melancholy

"What are you thinking, I asked Mom? I had just arrived at the nursing home and Mom was sitting in her wheelchair in the front parlor. I knew she recognized me because of the huge grin on her face revealing a mouth sans teeth. She sat speechless, staring at me as I walked up close and sat down on the couch beside her. Her face revealed a stare of conscious awareness as if she thought she know me, but wasn't sure.

I asked again. "What are you thinking about, Mom?"

She continued her gaze at me for a moment and then replied, "Nothing, I'm not thinking about anything."

Over the past few weeks I made a specific point of attempting to engage Mom in conversation. She appeared to be losing her incentive to communicate – losing her faculty to talk, losing any motivation to socialize, and losing mastery over her own life. It had to be the creeping dementia. There was no other explanation.

Mom always liked good conversation. An argument was ever better. She relished her ability at logical explanation. She delighted in the silence that ensued immediately following her retort to some comment she thought illogical and inane. I could see the look of "I've got you there" come over her face as she recognized her prowess in the arena of argument. That was before. Now there was only hollowness. Her eyes appeared sunken as if withdrawn from lack of interest and imagination. She just looked vacant. Conversation was minimal.

I asked questions not because I wanted to really know *what* she was thinking but because I wanted to know *if* she was thinking. If I knew what she was thinking, it might call for a response that invited intimacy. I wasn't ready for that. Just knowing that she still had thoughts, regardless of what they were, was enough.

It was hard for me to imagine a time, short of unconsciousness, sleep, or death, when a person is not thinking about something. I envisioned the brain as always active, never switched completely off, in a state of constant activity, sometimes with more momentum than other times, but never totally disengaged. The brain is perpetually active. It's always at work – remembering, analyzing, emoting, reviewing, planning, conniving, and scheming. Even when asleep, it's conjuring up dreams. When Mom says she is not thinking about anything, does she mean she isn't thinking at all or that what she is thinking about is of so little consequence that it's not worth recalling?

Lacking other resources to motivate her, I ask again. "What are you thinking about, Mom?"

She didn't look puzzled or baffled or curious about why I was asking. She just looked vacant.

Feeling adventurous, I ask, "Anything on your mind today?"

She looked at me with a glazed stare. "No, Nothing. I don't know what you are talking about."

I felt a need to ask probing questions, continuously seeking for some response to explore her consciousness. I wanted to be helpful. I wanted to intervene at the very point where I might make a difference, recapture some sense of her humanness that might still remain.

I recognized that loss, in all its manifestations, is a powerful emotion. Especially combined with dementia, if left unattended, severe loss can easily leave a person extremely vulnerable. Dementia has a way of positioning a person at one stage of life. Emotional growth is stymied. Socialization is halted. When communication ceases, marginalization and isolation threaten to overwhelm the person.

I wanted to gage Mom's circumstance, so I asked questions. I wanted Mom to tell her story.

"What do you remember about summers we spent at the beach?" I asked.

She began to looked puzzled as if to ask what I meant by the question. Then her blank look returned.

"Nothing." She responded.

"Do you remember when Ariel and I got married and you came to the wedding?"

"I suppose so."

I sensed a sign of hopefulness. "Well, what do you remember about the wedding?"

"What wedding? I don't know what you are talking about."

She showed no vestige of emotion, revealed no point of contact from which I could connect to enable her to express feelings. Without this faculty I felt completely at a loss for helping her regain some self-awareness, some connection with her spirituality. I knew something was there, but I couldn't coax it from her.

Losing your mind along with your memory has got to be the ultimate loss. Many times I have forgotten where I left my keys or address book. My family once lost a house in a hurricane. These are tragedies of small proportion. Things can be replaced. Losing your memory is losing your past, your history, your life. Dementia is more than tragedy. It's irreversible and irreplaceable.

7

A Time to Say Goodbye

"My mother is on some subterranean voyage, traveling towards death, making I know not what astonishing discoveries which she appears to have neither need nor desire to communicate.

It is as if she were on a spaceship beyond reach of telecommunications: One can only guess what kind of provisions she might require and try to provide them for her."...Simon Callow in *My Life in Pieces*

Mom eventually settled into a pattern. Her dementia had so overtaken her abilities that her participation in activities at the nursing home was at a minimum. She settled into routines. She sat by herself in the front room but only when she was able to conjure up enough inertia to get there by herself. She talked with no one. She continued to be assigned to the special dining area where staff supervised the meal times. I remember her sitting at a large half round table with five other residents, all in large bibs. They faced the staff assigned to the table who over saw the meal, making sure each resident didn't choke, didn't steal food from another's plate, and kept a log of what each person ate. She was among the fully dependent residents, those who the staff felt were incapable of fending for themselves.

Mom was not fully incapable. She still had some feistiness in her which revealed itself periodically. Her vocabulary was limited and she spoke rarely, but she still conjured up non-verbal ways to let others know what she wanted and how she felt. Many of the staff were surprised that she spoke as well as she did with me, as they rarely heard her speak when I was not around.

Mom and I were alone now. The nursing home staff met her basic needs – food, hygiene, medications – but it remained my task to provide for her social and emotional support. I was her entertainment, her family, the focus of her conversation, and the reason for her to get up each morning. There seemed no purpose to her life outside of daily meals and sleeping. She was approaching a vegetative existence. Her health remained steady. She didn't walk, she ate pureed food, and she remained incontinent. She no longer complained of nausea or cramps. Perhaps she did feel some physical pain but lacked the ability to communicate it.

Regular visits were a part of my agenda – every Wednesday and Sunday afternoon. Travel outside the nursing home became more and more difficult, but we still managed to get out. She loved riding in the car and going for ice cream, or at least she gave the impression that she did. To placate her, and as a way of attempting to provide some happiness and joy into her life, I encouraged these rides whenever possible.

Mom was now in her mid eighties, frail and bent over. She looked as if she could be easily broken with the slightest fall. Otherwise she remained resilient.

A wicked right hand

Mom never liked exercise. She thought it a waste of time. Any ailment that befell her - pains in her legs, stomach cramps, nausea, headaches - medicine was her preferred treatment, the more the better. The idea that physical exercise might alleviate pain and encourage body strength was alien to Mom.

Mom hated housework. Housework took physical agility and acumen. It annoyed her that if and when she did clean the house, it only got dirty again. She told us it was unnecessary and useless. When she did housework, it was more out of guilt than necessity.

Mom never held a job outside the home. She claimed it took all her energy to raise kids and cook dinner and do housework. She enjoyed her free time which was often spent reading, watching television or sleeping on the couch. She did not attempt to justify her actions; she didn't have to because the rest of our family feared starting an argument with Mom. It was a loosing experience.

What Mom did enjoy was often detrimental to her health. She over-indulged in sweets. She paid scant attention to diet. She drank too much. She shunned physical activity. This is not an indictment, but rather an observation. Knowing Mom's chosen life style helped me understand her dementia, her attitudes, and her emotions.

Mom was a verbal person. She abhorred work, but loved to talk. Most of her life, even into her golden years, she counted on her verbal skills to achieve her goals. She excelled at conversation, usually a one way conversation. She talked and you listened. She could easily hold her own in any debate and was prone toward argumentation. Once her mind was made up she was impossible to dissuade. Facts were not important, her insistence was paramount. She enjoyed having the last word. She had the power of gab and persuasion and didn't like being crossed.

Time, age, and dementia began to erode Mom's speech. It caused her great frustration. She found it difficult to communicate, especially how to tell people when she was annoyed or irritated. Communication became jumbled in her mind and her conversation skills lapsed. She knew what she wanted, but fumbled in her attempts to tell others.

Although her verbal skills might falter, her persistence didn't. She needed a substitute for language. When circumstances demanded it, she replaced talk with a wicked right hand. When her power of persuasion failed her verbally, she discovered an alternative – a swinging right hand slap.

Mom often elicited irritation with the nursing home routine. She balked at doing things according to someone else's schedule. She resisted forced baths when she wasn't ready. She refused the choice of dresses staff chose for her. She balked at changing her underwear when incontinent. When asked to move from directly in front of the television, she became belligerent. At the dinner table, if another resident sat in her accustomed seat, Mom would turn combative. Her weapon of choice was a wicked right hand.

She was fast and accurate. She caught the instigator by surprise. Before the other person realized her annoyance and prepared for defense, Mom's right hand lashed out, caught her alongside the head, and then recoiled. It all happened in a matter of nano seconds.

Mom didn't discriminate. When her favorite nurse aide who was pregnant accidentally pulled a sweater over Mom's head incorrectly, she felt the full force of Mom's right hand directly into her belly. If another resident violated Mom's space at the food table, a quick swipe of the right hand would lay across the offender's chest.

Mom would later suffer a mild stroke. While recuperating on a gurney at the local hospital, the nurse had to remove an intravenous needle from her arm. Mom didn't like that. We caught her arm just shy of whacking the nurse across the face.

Mom's intolerance of things that annoyed her increased with her age and was accentuated by her dementia. It must have been particularly upsetting to her to know what she wanted to say, but unable to say it. Her versatile range of verbal communication found its substitute, however, in her wicked right hand.

Stroke In the Park

"Can we get going now?" Mom interrupted me as I talked with one of the staff members. She began tugging on my shirt. Mom didn't like it when I was distracted. She expected that I was there to visit with her. She wanted my full attention.

"Let's get going." At least that's what I thought she said. Her speech had become extremely mumbled.

Mom insisted that we leave immediately.

"We need to go shopping now," she stated.

Mom was totally confined to a wheel chair. I had to lift her from under her arms and literally place her in the front seat of my pickup truck. She never complained about this "struggle" even though it must have somewhat painful.

She had poor posture and usually leaned to one side almost resting in my lap. Needless to say, this made driving difficult.

Our trips grew shorter each week; just enough time for her to have a cigarette, ice cream at the Dairy Queen, and to purchase some candy kisses at the drug store. They were routine trips, but Mom preferred it that way. She knew what to expect.

I stopped after leaving the parking lot to give Mom her usual cigarette. She inhaled it almost completely in one long breath and asked for another. I reluctantly obliged. She smoked the second one with just as much enthusiasm, but snuffed it out in the ash tray before it completely burned. She asked for another one. I refused. She sulked.

We were passing through the city park, Mom was exceptionally quiet, unusually so. Suddenly I noticed her hands and head began to shake, at first mildly, but then more violently.

"Mom," I shouted. "What's the matter?"

I watched her and the road intermittently at the same time. We were traveling slowly. She began to clench her fists tightly and stuck her arms straight out in front of her rigidly. Her upper body and then her legs stiffened and her head jerked backward until nearly her whole body went rigid. She started to slide down the front seat until her feet hit the fire wall under the dashboard. She appeared to be having difficulty breathing. Her eyes rolled up into her forehead.

I panicked. I thought she might be dying right there in the front seat of my truck. My gut reaction was to yell at her.

"Mom, damn it, sit up and start breathing right."

No response. She still looked rigid and clenched her fists ever more tightly. Her skin color was turning a light blue. I panicked. I had to get her to the hospital. I began driving as fast as possible through the park toward the local hospital, about three miles away.

I drove quickly but not recklessly. I didn't want to get stopped by a police officer and yet I did. I wondered which would be quicker, avoid the police and not waste time explaining or get stopped and asked the officer to accompany me to the hospital. I never saw an officer and arrived at the hospital emergency room door six minutes later.

I excitedly explained my predicament to the receptionist and immediately witnessed two attendants pushing a gurney toward the entrance. Mom was still in a semi-prone position in the front wedged between the front dashboard and the back of the front seat. She was stiff as a board. The attendants carefully, but promptly loaded her onto the gurney and wheeled her inside. They asked that I wait in the reception area. The receptionists asked if Mom had any insurance coverage.

Thirty minutes went by. A nurse came out and said I could visit with Mom. I noticed the color back in her face and she was breathing easily. She looked frightened and confused as she peered into my face. I don't think she was aware of what happened or where she was.

"Why am I here? What are they doing?" Mom asked me.

"You had a little accident," I told her.

"What are you talking about?" she asked.

"We'll talk about it when we get back home," I told her.

We remained in the emergency room about two hours. Nothing was done during that time and I am at a loss as to why they kept her so long after they finished treatment.

"We had to do some routine tests," a nurse explained to me. I didn't notice any procedures being done while I waited with Mom.

"What were you looking for?" I asked the nurse.

"Nothing in particular," she responded. "Just a precaution. She might have had a mild stroke and we want to be sure her heart is all right."

A few minutes later they dismissed us.

"Nothing conclusive," we were told. "We think she probably had a mild stroke. We don't see any after effects, so you can go home."

They escorted Mom outside in a wheelchair to my waiting truck. We started toward home.

"How are you feeling now," I asked. I wanted to be assured she was fine and ready to be at home.

"Fine," she replied. "Why do you keep asking that?" She sounded a bit annoyed. "Can I have another cigarette?"

Left Leaning

"Mom, why are you leaning so far over? You're going to fall out of the chair," I told her.

"I am not," she replied. "I don't know what you are talking about."

For the past few months, I noticed a distinct left leaning tendency whenever Mom was sitting in her wheelchair. It was even more pronounced when sitting at the meal table and in the front seat of my car. She leaned far over to her left side, not slumping forward or backward, but distinctly to the left. It looked as if she wanted to brace herself in a more comfortable position on the left using her left arm but it wasn't strong enough to hold her so she continued to slump further to the left. Sometimes her left leaning was so prominent that she fell over when nothing was there to stop her.

My wife told me that Mom's proneness for left leaning was probably a consequence of many factors. She had poor posture and weak muscles. She never exercised. Her dementia caused imbalance. She might be suffering the after effect from the mild stroke she had previously. That all sounded logical and consequential, but didn't relieve the annoyances I felt as she slumped to the left in my car.

Her condition was particular distracting when we went for rides. She slumped to the left so drastically that her head nearly rested in my lap. I tried propping her up with a pillow and some folded coats under her arm but that only caused her discomfort. She shoved the coats to the floor of the truck.

Her view was obstructed. From her left leaning position she could not see out the front or the side widows of the truck.

"Look Mom. There's a deer crossing the road," I told her as we rode through the park.

"Where? I don't see anything," she responded.

When viewing a scenic overlook, the changing colors of the trees, or the wildflowers, it was always too late if she tried to straighten up. We already passed the view. I couldn't stop if I was in traffic. It was pointless to explain to her that she was sitting in an awkward, left leaning position which caused her to miss seeing objects I pointed out as we passed by. She would respond, "You're crazy. I don't know what you are talking about."

I tried ways to correct her posture. I propped her in her wheelchair with pillows under her left side forcing her into a more upright position. At meal times, the staff person would scoot her chair under the table far enough so her elbows extended above the table. With her forearms on top of the table, she maintained in a more upright position. She ate with her right hand. Without help, it was difficult for her to reach her mouth so far over of the left. When nothing worked, I learned to cope with the situation.

Watching television presented a challenge. When leaning far to the left, she viewed the television sideways. Most time she no longer actively watched the television. She sat in the same room, and other residents just assumed she was watching. If I asked her what she was watching, she replied, "I don't know."

Mom didn't talk much so carrying on a conversation sideways didn't faze her. I noticed other residents and staff would begin to slant to the right to compensate when addressing. Most frustrating to me was that she seemed completely unaware of her severe left leaning tendencies. When she was reminded of her posture and when attempts were made to correct her, she acted very annoyed.

"Mom, you are slouching again. Can you sit up straight please," I often reminded her.

"I am not slouching," she said. "Stop pushing me. I don't know what you are talking about."

I reconciled myself to her awkward positioning. It appeared nothing would change.

Mom was scheduled for a medication review by her doctor. He suggested that a change in medications might prove helpful. Some of her medications were eliminated and some new ones prescribed. I asked about her medications, but didn't fully understand the explanations. The doctor simply described them as calming and preventative.

Drastic change happened overnight. The next day Mom sat upright, straight as an arrow for the first time in months. Movement in both arms vastly improved. Her ability to converse rallied. Her short term memory returned. She recognized people and called them by name. It was a wonderful restoration that I could hardly believe.

"How long might this last?" I asked the doctor.

"Can't tell, maybe permanently, maybe short term, but let me know what happens." He said.

I was so excited. I called my brothers with the good news.

"Mom is like a new person. It's almost like a miracle," I told them.

I encouraged them to visit while Mom had the gift of recognition and the willingness to gab. She could talk about things she remembered. They came and had a good visit.

I had to know so I asked Mom. "Mom, do you feel better now that you are sitting up straight? And your hands and arms; you use them so much better now. How does that make you feel?"

"How does what feel?" she asked. "I don't know what you are talking about."

And so it went for a few weeks. We had some good visits and some pleasant conversations so long as I didn't ask "any stupid questions." But the end came quickly. Within a month, Mom started her descent to the left once again. Along with the left leaning came also the lapse in memory. Conversation waned almost completely. It seemed the deeper she slouched the more her memory declined and her awareness evaporated. Medications were adjusted once again, but there was no improvement this time.

"How do you explain this" I asked the doctor. "Last time there was an almost immediate improvement and this time nothing."

"I think her dementia has gotten too deep and ingrained for the medications to alleviate her symptoms. Remember, I told you maybe yes and maybe no. No guarantees," he said.

I wondered if it was really the medications or simply a stirring of her will that caused the profound improvement. She rallied for a short time as if she had some experience she yet wanted to have before the end, one final desire to know her family as she had always known them.

Letting Go of Mom

The Phone rang at 3:30 A.M. It startled me from a deep sleep. I thought I was dreaming and hesitated to answer it. When I realized it was real, I jumped out of bed hoping I could reach the phone before my wife was awakened. I stumbled in the dark, bumping my knee against the desk while looking for my glasses. I needed my glasses. I can't talk on the phone without "seeing" whom, I am talking with.

"Hello," I said

"Is this Mr. Olsen," a voice replied.

"Yes."

"Mr. Olsen, this is the night nurse at Eden Home." Immediately, I sensed there was a problem with Mom. She probably fell out of bed again or wet her sheets and wouldn't cooperate with the staff and hit one of the nurse aides. "Your mother, Roberta, has a serious problem. She has been vomiting and there appears to be some blood there. And her intestines, at least we think it's her intestines, are coming out her vagina. We think we need to get her to the hospital right away. I have called for an ambulance."

I thought I heard what she said, but I asked her to repeat it again. She did and it sounded unbelievable.

"Her intestines are coming out her vagina, is that what you said?" I asked. "How could that be? Yes, get her to the hospital right away."

I hung up.

I called the hospital emergency room and explained what I heard from the nursing home. I asked if they would call me as soon as Mom arrived. We would meet her there. My wife was now awake and we both started to get dressed. The phone rang a second time.

"Peter, this is Dr. Flannigan. Your mother is here right now and I need to know how aggressive you want us to be? There is about three feet of her intestine protruding from her vagina. It's really serious."

I asked him to hold off for fifteen minutes. We were on our way.

At the emergency room, different doctors advised us. She could have immediate surgery or be left alone. Surgery, they said, was not a good option. Mom's age and condition made the procedure risky with scant assurance it would resolve much. The second option meant she was on her own and survival or not was entirely up to her. Both doctors concurred that survival either way might be short lived.

The idea that Mom's intestines were poking out her vagina seemed surreal, almost bizarre. How could a person's intestines just slip out? Intestines are an internal organ, protected by body parts. They don't just empty themselves like a waste basket. I conjured up images of children's stories where the gangster lay on the sidewalk with his "guts" hanging out, the ultimate symbol of complete annihilation. I didn't understand how Mom could survive such an episode.

"What about any pain?" I asked the doctors.

"She should be fine. We can keep her pain free in the hospital," the told me. "Morphine works real well."

I didn't hold much hope that Mom would be a good patient. Even under sedation, I imagined her being intolerant of feeding tubes and intravenous medications. She would be prone to pulling them out. Her dementia would contribute to her uncooperative nature. I wished that she would die right there on the emergency room examination table. I kept these thoughts to myself.

Mom was admitted to the hospital as a hospice patient. Her diagnosis was terminal. I just didn't know when. I trusted hospice. They had kept my father pain free and I felt assured they would do the same for Mom.

I became anxious as I watched Mom's breathing the first day in the hospital. It was slow and laborious. Breathing seemed like a struggle for her. I kept listening intently, thinking it had stopped on a number of occasions, only to revive. I wanted it to stop.

She lay on her side with restraints on her arms to keep her from grabbing her intestines. She barely moved. Occasionally she flailed her arms only to the extent the restraints allowed. These movements seemed like acts of desperation, non-verbal communication of her discomfort. The hospice nurse assured me she was comfortable.

"How do you know that?" I asked. "She doesn't look comfortable when she struggles with her arms."

"Because her breathing is peaceful and her lungs are not congested. Movements are normal," she told me. I wondered if that was a standard speech meant to appease me. "Besides, she is getting enough morphine to calm a cow."

I remembered being told that Morphine will hasten the dying process. Once it's introduced, each succeeding dose needs to be stronger and the stronger the dosage, the greater the burden on the vital body functions.

I could see Mom's eyes moving under her closed lids. An occasional twitching of facial muscles and flailing of her restrained arms remained her only movements. She never looked at me or responded to my voice.

How quickly the transition from being fully alive; hungry, sleeping, watching television, going for rides, walking in her wheelchair, and yelling at the staff to motionless, barely breathing, semi-conscious, and awaiting death. I had grown so used to Mom's routine. I expected each visit to be the same as the last visit, nothing different, always the same, forever and ever. Yesterday she was my mother. Today, she seemed distant, someone I hardly knew, a body quickly deteriorating with her intestines hanging out.

I put my face close to her mouth to hear if her breathing had stopped. I hoped that it had, but she gasped another breath. Her skin was blotchy. The needle in her arm continued to provide minimal nourishment. A separate needle filled her with morphine for pain and other medications to settle her stomach so she wouldn't choke on her own sputum. Restraints still held her arms so she would not reach for her bowels. The thought of her being alive under these circumstances made me shudder. I was glad she remained unconscious.

"Please, Mom, stop breathing," I said out loud.

Friends stopped by. They asked how she was doing. They really wanted to know my mental state. I tried acting remorseful, but just wanted her to stop breathing. I wondered if she was thinking. Can a person continue to think when lying in a coma?

I thought about the difference between birth and death. Birth seems so predictable and accurate. Nine months of gestation and out comes the baby, ready or not. Death felt like it took forever. Birth is a purposeful event. It's planned. It's expected. It comes with great hopes and expectations. Death seems to have no meaningful results. It's not expected. It's to be avoided. Watching someone die is an act requiring great patience.

Mom died the next day. She passed on while we were present. My wife and I said goodbye. I wondered if she heard our voices. I wondered what she was thinking about.

8

Bidding Mom Adieu

"If we have been pleased with life, we should not be displeased with death, since it comes from the hand of the same master."...Michelangelo

There are no "do overs" for death. A funeral is a once in a life time experience. You get it right the first time or forget about it.

Funerals are forever, the last and final expression of honor. I remember being told by a friend that the best way to determine the worth of person is by the number of people who show up for their funeral. Only seven people showed up for my mother's funeral. Four of us were family. The other three were strangers.

I felt betrayed. Mixed emotions ran through me; disappointment, sadness, frustration and anger. I tried to rationalize that the lack of adoration expressed toward my mother was not a reflection of my personal worth or value. Nonetheless, the absence of people was a blow to my pride and aroused feelings of despair.

Death has a way of resolving all issues. Mom was not bothered. She had passed the point of being judgmental. It was now my problem. I felt very uncomfortable in that huge church sanctuary employing two able pastors to celebrate the life and death of Mom with only seven people present. It felt like a travesty, a slap in the face to her and to me.

Invitations are not sent to attend a funeral. It's not like inviting people to a birthday party of anniversary celebration.

There are no cards with enclosed RSVP's. E-mails seem undignified.

Funerals are announced publicly – in the newspaper, from church pulpits, by people who know. The word gets spread. There was no newspaper obituary. It cost too much. Nothing was said in her church congregation. I don't remember telling anyone other than family about the date and time for the service. It was my mistake, yet, I still felt that people should have known, should have been there.

People show up for funerals to be seen. They want the community to know them as compassionate people. Respect shown to the dearly departed is a measure of esteem for the survivors. It scores big points with the dead person's family. Seven people hardly qualify as a measure of care or consideration. No points were scored at Mom's funeral.

My brothers' lived too far away or simply choose not to come. Aunts and uncles were too old to travel. Nephews and nieces all had other obligations. Pop, her husband, had died two years previously. Mom had no friends. The few she once had were already dead or lived long distances away. So no one came, except the seven of us, myself, my wife and my two daughters, and three people who came late who I didn't know and sat behind us.

It felt awkward to be so alone for this final tribute, an occasion that could not be postponed or repeated on another more convenient day. Perhaps my expectations were too idealistic and unfounded. Mom was a stranger in this community and her dementia prevented her from making new friends in the nursing home. That's a rational excuse, but emotionally I felt otherwise.

Mom was not a celebrity, she was unknown. She did not live an extraordinary life. She didn't paint pictures or write novels. She wasn't president of a club or civic organization. She abhorred sports, except for one time when she decided Ice skating would be good exercise. That didn't last long. She once organized dance lesson for my middle school and hosted a Halloween party at our church and, for a short time, volunteered at our local library. She loved to read. These activities were not notable enough to entice a crowd. Until dementia overcame her, her life was anything but bizarre or eccentric so her funeral didn't appeal to the curious.

She nurtured three sons who provided her with seven grandchildren and two great grandchildren. Her dementia robbed her of the ability to remember them and she didn't recognize them when they visited. Still, I could not dismiss the irrational expectation that people would want to pay tribute at her funeral. I was mistaken.

I tried to explain away why no one came to her funeral. Perhaps they felt her dementia was a contagious disease and they feared catching it. But she wasn't sick. She died of old age. Perhaps she had offended people by her actions or words. She hardly spoke the last few years. Maybe people held old grudges. But she lived an isolated life the last ten years and rarely left the nursing home. Who could she have affronted? No, I think it was that she became invisible. No body knew her. She just didn't exist. She had been forgotten, ignored. That would explain their absence. It wasn't intentional. It was ignorance.

I had friends. I lived in the community for twenty years and thought myself well respected and highly regarded. If these friends didn't know Mom, they knew me. Didn't they feel any obligation to support me? I was wrong again.

No, it must be Mom's fault. I blamed her. She was the cause of my embarrassment and disappointment. If she had put forth more effort toward achieving something significant during her life - accomplished something great or notable, acquired wealth, written a book, been president of an organization, anything besides being just "Bert", my mother, the woman with dementia - there would have been hundreds of people at her funeral. They would have clamored to be "seen" at the service, be recognized as a friend of Bert, the "special" woman. Knowing influential people is contagious. It nurtures one's self-importance and builds one's ego. That wasn't a rational thought and I stopped being angry at Mom.

It must be my fault. I coerced my parents to move from their last home by telling them how much better it would be to live near me and in the assisted living facility. I never thought about their spirituality, that they might thrive better by controlling their own destiny, draw significance from the familiar, or find security in the way they always did things. I uprooted them and moved them across the country to unfamiliar surroundings. Where they used to live they had friends and memories and I took that all away from them.

I took away their self-responsibility. Their guardianship was entrusted to me, but only reluctantly. No longer were they responsible for themselves. I knew, but altogether ignored, that when that happens, it's an omen of anticipated and complete abdication. Loss of self-control changes attitudes drastically. Self-reliance becomes abandoned without self-control. Personal initiative and motivation soon gives way to acquiescence and resignation. Giving in and giving up happens expeditiously. Did I take their self-respect by taking their self-responsibility? These thoughts permeated my consciousness as I contemplated that so few people came to Mom's funeral.

Mom was cremated. The funeral director assured me that a box with her remains would be ready by Monday morning. I trusted that the ashes in the box would be hers. I wondered how I would know for sure. The service was planned for Monday afternoon. It didn't matter much that I get back her remains on time since it was to be a memorial service. Mom wasn't required to be present.

Mom wasn't very religious. She never actively opposed matters of the spirit. I don't think she was an atheist. She just was not very interested. "This God stuff," she liked to say, "just didn't matter much." She did enjoy, however, an occasional conversation, especially if it could be turned into a debate, over whether God really existed or simply invented to fill a void in our knowledge of the ethereal. She leaned toward the invention theory.

Attending church was not her thing. A few times, when the Women's Circle needed help sewing clothing for the annual doll sale, she consented. She enjoyed the chats she had with the other women more than the sewing. I never witnessed her reading the bible, but she was aware of the biblical mandate of "ashes to ashes, dust to dust" and proclaimed on many occasion that concept made sense to her. She insisted on cremation. Long before she acquired dementia, she asked that her ashes be scattered on the beach of Fire Island, New York, a place she claimed held many joyous memories for her.

Mom showed me a piece of paper some time ago that indicated she wanted her body parts donated to science after her death before being cremated. She didn't stipulate exactly what parts of her body qualified or to which branch of science they was to go. I never asked. At first I thought seriously of honoring her request. It seemed a noble gesture. What she did not achieve in life might be amended in death. Perhaps some great medical insight might evolve into some life-extending discovery.

I decided against doing this. Two reasons were compelling. First, I assumed her body had been pretty well used up and decimated by her constant sicknesses and the debilitation brought on by excessive smoking, drinking, and general lack of physical care. She was never a well person. Secondly, and most important, I felt revulsion with the idea of her eyes plucked out of her head, her brain dislodged and dissected, and her innards sent off to some obscure laboratory to be examined by an anonymous researcher. It felt like a violation of what little sanctity remained for Mom.

Cremation was the way to go. It felt like an act of contrition, a penitence for the abuse of the gift of life given to her. I gleaned from brief conversations, perhaps partly imagined and partly rationalized, that Mom did acknowledge that life was a gift, possibly from God, created out of nothing. It was her intention, I supposed, that when life was over, it was proper to return the gift to show gratitude. She was born from nothing, she shall return to nothing. Ashes to ashes, dust to dust. What goes around comes around. I felt comfortable bringing Mom's ashes and not Mom to the church that Monday morning.

The minister of my church met Mom while he roamed the halls of the nursing home. His acquaintance was limited to "hello's" and "how are yous?" The resident chaplain faired better, but only marginally. She could recognize Mom in a group of people but had never actually spoken with her. It felt awkward to ask them to conduct a service of remembrance for someone they didn't know. I asked anyway, and they graciously consented. The only alternative was to conduct the service myself.

"Can we meet together so I can tell you some things about Mom, where she was born, what she liked to do, some tidbits about her personality," I asked them?

"Not to worry," they told me. "We can do the service. We are professionals."

Although I got no direct refusal, I didn't get any encouragement either. They seemed unconcerned about details of Mom's life and I was not asked to contribute unsolicited information. I figured that meant they would provide the "standard Christian burial service," which comes with a smattering of genuine prayers of supplication, appropriate bible verses, bona fide heartfelt empathy, and sincere words of condolence for the grieving family. I was assured that both ministers would be present and prepared by 2:00 P.M. Monday. The honorarium was one hundred dollars for each. Sincerity seemed at a minimum.

A few minutes before two o'clock, my wife, my two daughters, and I entered from the rear of the church. We walked past empty pews and took our seats in the front. The sanctuary was massive and ornate. The solid oak pews were aligned in orderly fashion and could accommodate six hundred people. Stained glass windows, each depicting a different episode in the life of Jesus, extended from floor to ceiling every few feet around the inside perimeter of the building. Red carpet graced the main isle from front to back. Huge pillars held up the cathedral ceiling. A massive wooden cross graced the alter area. It was bereft of flowers. I had forgotten to order some.

I looked back frequently toward the entrance expecting others to enter. Despite my attempt to appear solemn, I felt my anxiety rising.

"Maybe people are caught in traffic," I said to my wife.

"Yes, perhaps," she said.

I could feel a sense of sadness overcome me as I contemplated that we might be all alone. Where are my friends? Do I have any friends? Feelings of abandonment and hurt began to well up inside me. The absence of people felt like a personal rejection. Because my friends failed me, I failed my mother.

My daughter sensed my anxiety.

"Don't worry about it Dad," she reassured me. "What's important is that you are here and we support you. If nobody else comes we can still say we gave grandma a good send off."

She gave my hand a squeeze and smiled up at me. It felt comforting. Okay. I was ready.

The clergy worked diligently at being devout and reverent. They took turns reading biblical texts – "*In my Father's house are many mansions and I go to prepare a place for you*," and then "*Yea though I walk through the valley of the shadow of death, I fear no evil*" – words of solace and comfort. At that moment I didn't feel the need for release from grieving, I needed consolation from humiliation. I needed soothing for my anger. I was hung up in the thought that Mom's worth, my worth, was measured in direct proportion to the lack of people at the service. I couldn't concentrate on Mom's departure. I was distracted by my own hurt and rejection, my own distress and abandonment.

The clergy continued. "To live for the Lord is to live in the Lord. Roberta was truly a woman who lived for the Lord. In God's sight, death is never in vain." I wondered where they got this stuff. Did they truly feel they were reflecting Mom's faith or was it all generic theology?

Suddenly there was a disruption from the back of the sanctuary. Three women quietly walked into the church and sat down a few pews behind us. I turned and smiled politely. I didn't recognize them but wanted to extend a welcome.

The ministers got personal. They made up stories about pleasant conversations they had with Mom. It was generic small talk.

"Roberta always had a smile on her face. She impressed me with the tidbits of wisdom she was able to impart. She had such a vibrant personality," the chaplain stated.

"Such devotion to her family. She oozed dignity despite such overwhelming challenges," the other minister said.

"What challenges are you talking about? What vibrant personality?" I wondered.

When the clergy ran out of accolades, they asked if family members wanted to share thoughts or memories about Roberta.

There was silence in the sanctuary. My wife and daughters looked to me as if saying; "Now it's your turn dad." I felt unprepared and caught off guard.

My oldest daughter broke the awkward silence.

"I remember the time when Grandma choked on the turkey at Thanksgiving. We had to apply the Heimlich maneuver on her," she said. "Grandma was so excited about being there and getting some real turkey meat that she forgot how to chew. After she choked, she immediately grabbed another piece and we had to restrain her."

More memories came pouring out.

"Remember the time she landed face first in the grass after her wheel chair went rolling down the hill – with her in it?" my other daughter said. "When dad lost his grip on the chair, I though we had lost her for sure. I remember how indignant she was. She wasn't hurt, just annoyed. Remember how she asked to get back home so she could have another cigarette?"

And them I chimed in.

"I can still see her face that day I visited and she smiled so broadly that her front dentures fell right out of her mouth. She didn't even notice. She used to lose her teeth all the time and we would find them in the strangest places, under the bed, in a different room, one time even in the toilet bowl."

Our memories flourished as we recalled more hilarious recollections about Mom. Most seemed ordinary, perhaps upsetting when they occurred, but now they brought back fond memories. No disrespect was intended. The stories gave the impression of a family reunion when people talk about the strange uncle, make innocent jokes, tell tall tales, and perhaps embellish a bit. It was done with fondness.

While we rambled on, the ministers and the three guests who I now recognized as nursing home staff listened intently. Their fixed stares and open mouths, however, gave the impression they didn't share in the merriment but rather thought of us as most irreverent and disrespectful of the dearly departed. It could be they thought we hadn't an ounce of empathy toward Mom or that we always acted shamefully, crass, and outrageous.

We were telling it like we witnessed it. It came as a release, a catharsis, a moment of venting pent up stress. It felt appropriate. Mom wouldn't have been offended. She suffered greatly, but now death itself had passed, and there were some lighter moments along the journey that needed to be remembered. Mom was a bit irreverent herself.

When the clergy had enough storytelling, they interrupted us, asked that we pray with them, and then ended with "Let Roberta go so God can take her. May your grief be wholesome and welcomed." Grief was not a prominent feeling. I suspected I would miss her, but at the moment I felt relief that she no longer suffered. It was not a sorrowful time. I felt as if a burden had been lifted. Mom's life was completed, no more anticipating what might become of her. No more worries or anxieties or interruptions in my life because of her. I recognized the selfishness but also the truth.

I don't know if Mom welcomed death or feared it. We never spoke about that. It was a family characteristic that we not reveal feelings. If she had any anxieties or fears or expectations, she never spoke of them. The dementia left her without much ability to expresses herself. I could only hope that she had reconciled with the thought of death.

The clergy concluded the service with "sincere" handshakes and pats on the back and the words, "I'm sorry about your Mom, but she's in a better place now." I wasn't sorry about her death. I had hoped for Mom's death for the past two years. I could only imagine the embarrassment she must have felt at having to wear diapers, eating "already chewed" food, sleeping in her wheel chair and falling out, smiling with no teeth, mumbling to other residents, being denied cigarettes, and treated as if she were a two - year - old child. I hoped death would come to relieve her of these indignities. Her dementia robbed her of self-reliance. Self-consciousness seemed elusive. Her inability to communicate made it impossible to know if she achieved a sense of contentment or peace in her life. Death was her saving grace.

Mom's memorial service marked a watershed in my life. Both parents were gone and I was no longer "burdened" with the responsibility of care taker. No longer would I feel resentful because they expected too much or guilty for not doing enough. Or at least so I thought. One does not easily abandon reflections of lives lived. Although this chapter ended, the next one is just beginning. Closure now gives me the time for reflection, time to consider the mistakes I made, and time has its way of wishing for second chances. I wish more people would have been present for Mom's final celebration, but that wasn't her fault. I can't do that over.

I know that I am a better person for having had this tumultuous relationship with my parents this last decade of their lives. I chose to take this responsibility, and I don't feel I was neglectful. But time provides a new perspective. Like it or not, a person needs to re-examine the relationship and to re-consider how it could have been better "if only." It is the "if onlies" that I would like to have a chance to do over again, if not for my parents' benefit, then surely for my own.

www.ingramcontent.com/pod-product-compliance
Lightning Source LLC
Chambersburg PA
CBHW071439090426
42737CB00011B/1717